IQ
BOOSTERS

More than 300
Mind-Blowing Puzzles

STEVE RYAN

STERLING INNOVATION
An imprint of Sterling Publishing Co., Inc.

New York / London
www.sterlingpublishing.com

STERLING, the distinctive Sterling logo, STERLING INNOVATION and the Sterling Innovation logo
are registered trademarks of Sterling Publishing Co., Inc.

Library of Congress Cataloging-in-Publication Data Available

2   4   6   8   10   9   7   5   3   1

Published by Sterling Publishing Co., Inc.
387 Park Avenue South, New York, NY 10016

© 2009 by Sterling Publishing Co., Inc.

This book is comprised of material from the following Sterling titles:
Pencil Puzzlers © 1992 by Steve Ryan
Test Your Puzzle IQ © 1993 by Steve Ryan
Test Your Math IQ © 1994 by Steve Ryan
Mystifying Math Puzzles © 1996 by Steve Ryan

Distributed in Canada by Sterling Publishing
c/o Canadian Manda Group, 165 Dufferin Street
Toronto, Ontario, Canada M6K 3H6
Distributed in the United Kingdom by GMC Distribution Services
Castle Place, 166 High Street, Lewes, East Sussex, England BN7 1XU
Distributed in Australia by Capricorn Link (Australia) Pty. Ltd.
P.O. Box 704, Windsor, NSW 2756, Australia

Printed in China
All rights reserved

Sterling ISBN 978-1-4027-6007-5

For information about custom editions, special sales, premium and
corporate purchases, please contact Sterling Special Sales
Department at 800-805-5489 or specialsales@sterlingpublishing.com.

Contents

A NOTE TO THE READER

Put on your thinking caps and prepare to explore a macrocosm of mathematical puzzles, posers, pastimes, and paradoxes. Mathematics isn't just quantum theory. It takes the form of such popular contests as tic-tac-toe and chess. Galileo once described mathematics as the alphabet in which God has created the universe.

Before you is a competitive arena for the mind in which the rewards are great self-satisfaction. Much of the fun and fascination of solving mathematical diversions is derived from applying the precise logic that restores order to the chaos of a problem. With a little creative cunning you can restore harmony to these mathematical mind benders.

I often think of my puzzles as a bridge between mathematics and art. Each puzzle is aesthetically designed to capture the eye, flirt with the curiosity, and tempt your thought processes to follow a thread of reason on a meandering journey of mathematical delight. Some puzzles ask you to apply the basics: addition, subtraction, multiplication, and division; others require more abstract mathematical maneuvers, manipulations, and meditation. There are magic squares, devious dissections, tessellation teasers, problems in topology, and much more.

If you're up to the challenge, and I'm sure you are, you're in for a terrific think test and hours of fun. For, whether you're a "Mathemagician" or a "Number Novice," all of these puzzles are guaranteed to intrigue.

So sharpen your pencils, and sharpen your wits. You may be a lot more mathwise than you think!

STEVE RYAN

1

Test Your MATH IQ

1.

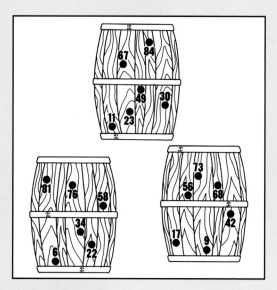

BEER BARREL POKER

Each of these barrels contains 100 gallons of beer. Can you poke out a knothole in each barrel to leave a total of exactly 100 gallons in all three barrels combined? The number at each knothole shows the gallons that would remain in the given barrel.

Solution on page 320.

2.

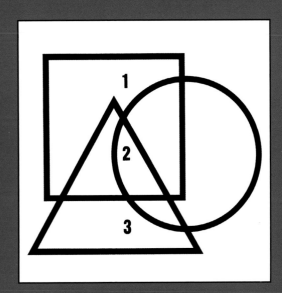

PUT IN SHAPE

Place the remaining numbers from 1 to 10 in the seven divisions of this overlapping geometric configuration to fulfill the following requirements:
1) The circle, square, and triangle must individually total thirty.
2) The three outer divisions of the circle, square, and triangle must also total thirty.

Solution on page 321.

(Need a clue? Turn to page 14.)

3.

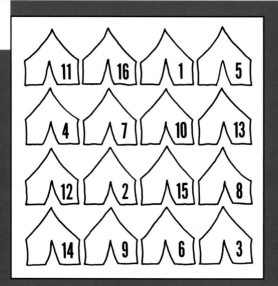

IN TENTS

It is known that four officers are strategically located in four different tents that total thirty-two. Orders state that each horizontal, vertical, and diagonal row of four tents must quarter one officer. Which tents do the officers occupy?

Solution on page 323.

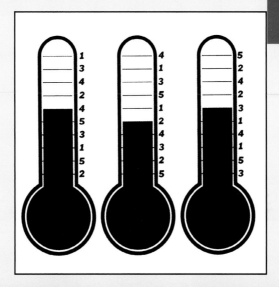

THE
THIRD
DEGREE

Your challenge is to balance the thermometers in this puzzle in such a way that they all read an identical number. For each unit rise in any thermometer, one of the other thermometers must fall one unit, and vice versa.

Solution on page 325.

5.

CANDY CODED

It is known that each horizontal, vertical, and diagonal row of four candies totals 200 calories. You must determine the calorie content of each piece of candy from the following information:

> Three candies have 20 calories apiece.
> Two candies have 40 calories apiece.
> Seven candies have 60 calories apiece.
> Three candies have 80 calories apiece.
> The black candy is calorie-free.

Solution on page 327.

6.

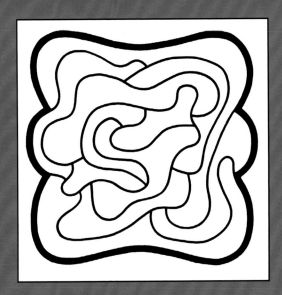

SHADY
HOLLOWS

There are eleven hollow shapes in this puzzle. It is your challenge to shade in four shapes that do not border one another.

Solution on page 329.

MAD HATTER'S
CAP SIZE

Here is a puzzle in which your challenge is to eliminate fractions. Add two or more of the cap sizes together to produce a whole number.

Solution on page 331.

(Need a clue? Turn to page 17.)

Clue to puzzle 2: One division remains blank.

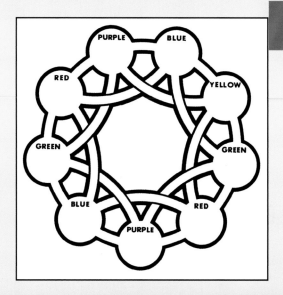

TRUE TO ONE'S COLORS

The interior lines of this puzzle crisscross but do not intersect. Place the numbers 1 through 9 in the nine colored circles to fulfill the following requirements: 1) Any set of three numbers that totals fifteen (there are eight) must include three different colors. 2) Numbers of consecutive value may not be directly linked by any passage.

Solution on page 320.

WICKED NUMBERS

The numbers 1 through 9 appear three times each in this puzzle. Your assignment is to blow out three candles that will total fifteen in each of the three horizontal rows. The three candles you select must carry the numbers 1 through 9. (No number may be used more than once.)

Solution on page 321

(Need a clue? Turn to page 20.)

10.

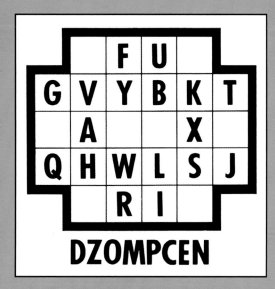

DZOMPCEN

NIGHTWALKER

Position the eight remaining letters of the alphabet in the vacant squares of this puzzle to complete an alphabetical progression created by the moves of a chess knight.

Solution on page 323.

Clue to puzzle 7:
Try "capsizing" one of the hats.

11.

MAGIC
WORD SQUARES

Each letter in this puzzle represents a different number from 0 to 9. It is your challenge to switch these letters back to numbers in such a way that each horizontal, vertical, and diagonal row of three words totals the same number. Your total for this puzzle is 1,446.

Solution on page 325.

(Need a clue? Turn to page 21.)

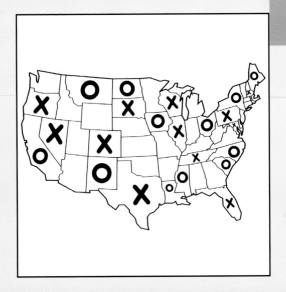

TIC-TAC-TOPOLOGY

Here's a strategy game of topology for two players. Simply force your opponent to connect three or more states with their Xs or Os and you win the game. Just as in tic-tac-toe, one player plays X and one player plays O. Players alternate positioning one of their marks per state until one player is forced to connect three or more states. In this sample game in progress, it is your move and challenge to position an O on the map in such a way that it will be impossible for your opponent to position an X without losing the game. Note: Only one X or O can be used to mark Michigan (a bridge is shown connecting both halves), but diagonally adjacent states, such as Arizona and Colorado, are not considered connected. You can enjoy playing this game with maps of other countries and continents.

Solution on page 327.

13.

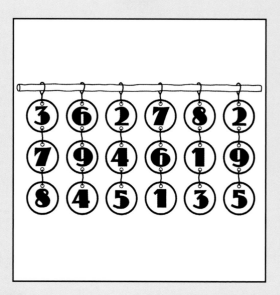

HANG BY
A THREAD

Each of the numbers 1 through 9 appears twice in the eighteen disks that are hanging by threads. Your task is to cut the least number of threads so as to drop one set of numbers and leave nine disks hanging that reveal the remaining set of numbers from 1 to 9.

Solution on page 329.

Clue to puzzle 9:
Start by blowing out the middle candle.

14.

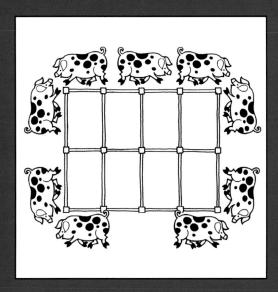

PIG STYMIE

Put nine pigs in eight pens.

Solution on page 331.

Clue to puzzle 11: APE = 473.

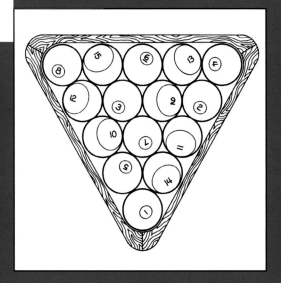

RACK YOUR BRAIN

An interesting game of pool involving three players has just been completed. It has a winner, but the total point scores are as close as possible. Determine how the balls were distributed from the following information: 1) Each player has a different number of balls. 2) No player has two balls of consecutive number. 3) No player has two balls of identical color.

Ball colors: 1 and 9 are yellow, 2 and 10 are blue, 3 and 11 are red, 4 and 12 are purple, 5 and 13 are orange, 6 and 14 are green, 7 and 15 are maroon, 8 is black.

Solution on page 320.

(Need a clue? Turn to page 25.)

SQUARE
DESPAIR

Make two straight cuts that divide this figure into four pieces of equal size and shape which, when rearranged, will form a square revealing another square within.

Solution on page 322.

(Need a clue? Turn to page 30.)

17.

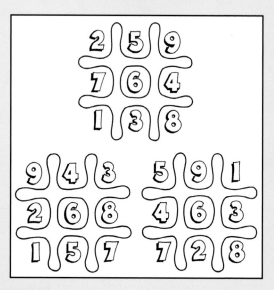

TIC-TAC-TOTAL

Your challenge in this puzzle is to circle a winning tic-tac-toe on each of the three game boards in the following manner: 1) One game must contain a diagonal win, one game must contain a horizontal win, and one game must contain a vertical win. 2) All numbers from 1 through 9 must be circled in constructing these three winning lines.

Solution on page 325.

18.

MENTAL
BLOCKS

At present, the numbers 49,067 and 58,132 appear in these ten mental blocks. Can you switch the positions of any two blocks to create two new numbers so that one number will be twice as large as the other?

Solution on page 327.

Clue to puzzle 15: The player with the highest score has the least number of balls.

SAUCER SORCERY

The sorcerer's symbols are the lightning bolt, the crescent moon, and the star. Each symbol has a specific amount of magical power. The saucers in this puzzle reveal the magnitude of those powers. It is known that the three crisscrossing arrows point to saucers of equivalent powers. Your task is to determine which symbol or symbols, equaling the star, must be positioned in the empty saucer.

Solution on page 330.

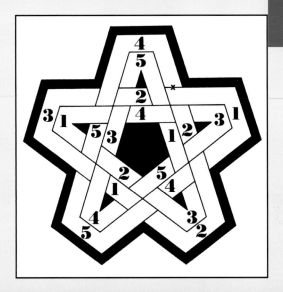

SIRIUS
BUSINESS

Cross out or remove sixteen of the short divider lines of this puzzle (one is given) in such a way that four large shapes, each containing the numbers 1 through 5, are formed.

Solution on page 331.

21.

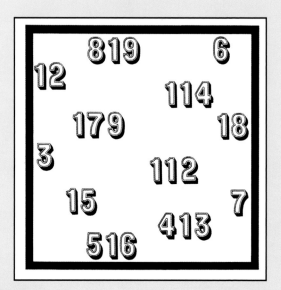

**PERFECT
PERFECT
VISION**

Using four straight lines, divide this square into nine pieces so that each piece totals the same number.

Solution on page 322.

22.

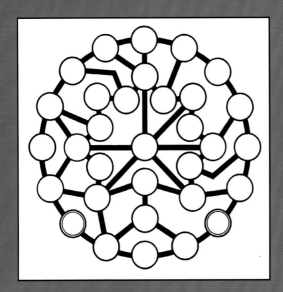

FAIR IS WHEEL

Here is a puzzle that offers two ways to solve. Your challenge is to trace two paths that contain an "even" number of total rings beginning and ending at the double rings. Your first path must be the shortest possible route, and your second path must be the longest possible route. No ring or connector may be used more than once per solution.

Solution on page 323.

PAINTIN' PLACE

A painter has five ten-gallon paint cans containing consecutive gallon amounts of each color. From the following information, how many gallons of each color are left in each can? 1) There are eight gallons total of red and green paint. 2) There are ten gallons total of blue and yellow paint. 3) There are thirteen gallons total of green, yellow, and orange paint. 4) There are nine gallons total of red, blue, and orange paint.

Solution on page 325.

Clue to puzzle 16: Strangely, the area of the negative space created by the interior square will be greater than the area of the original shape.

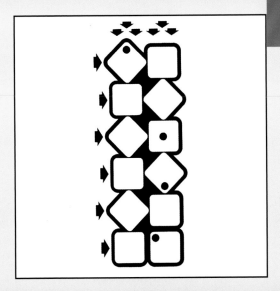

SEVENS
THE
HARD
WAY

These six pairs of regulation dice have most of their pips missing. It is your task to position the missing pips to fulfill the following requirements: 1) Each of the six stacked pairs of dice must total seven. 2) Each of the six vertical pip columns pointed out by the six arrows at the top must also total exactly seven pips. 3) Both vertical towers of six dice must reveal all faces, one through six.

Solution on page 328.

25.

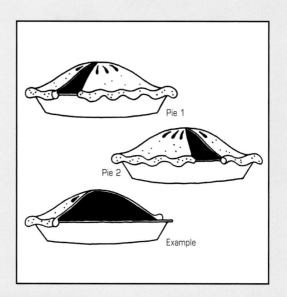

Pie 1

Pie 2

Example

PIE CENTENNIALS

Each of the three pies above has been cut into two pieces with the smaller piece removed. Using the bottom pie as an example, the smaller piece measures $47^{3/6}$ percent of the pie, and the larger piece measures $52^{9/18}$ percent. Together they total exactly 100 percent of the pie and utilize all nine numbers 1 through 9. Your task is to illustrate the piece sizes of the two remaining pies in the same manner. As in the example, all pieces must be made up of no less than four numbers and no more than five numbers. In the first pie, it is known that the smaller piece is less than five percent. In the second pie, it is known that the smaller piece is greater than eight percent.

          Solution on page 330.

26.

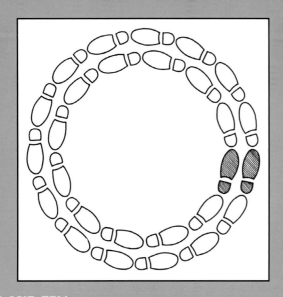

SHOE AND TELL

Here is a puzzle that will literally have you walking in circles. Start your circular stroll with both feet on the shaded footprints. Beginning with the right foot, walk in a normal manner, always stepping to the next marked print. Never skip a footprint. If each footstep measures 10 inches, how many steps are required before a stride of 52½ inches is reached?

Solution on page 331.

(Need a clue? Turn to page 39.)

27.

STAR STUDIED

There are ten stars in this puzzle. You are to color eighty percent of the stars blue and seventy percent of the stars red. That means that fifty percent of the stars must be both blue and red. The stars must also be colored in such a way that two straight lines can be drawn to divide the stars into three groups: one in which the stars are all blue, one in which the stars are all red, and one in which the stars are both blue and red.

Solution on page 320.

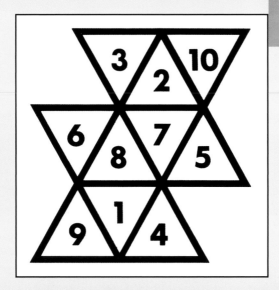

DEVIL TRIANGLES

In this sample puzzle, the numbers 1 through 10 have been so positioned that each group of four small triangles creates a larger triangle totaling twenty-two. There are four such overlapping triangles. It is your task to find four additional solutions for this puzzle, each of which must have different totals.

Solution on page 322.

(Need a clue? Turn to page 45.)

29.

WEAVE
ONLY JUST BEGUN

The weave in this puzzle is not complete. When completed it will divide this puzzle into three separate paths. Eight key crossovers are already drawn in. Your task is to complete the remaining sixteen of the twenty-four overcrossings so that each strand will total exactly 100.

Solution on page 324

30.

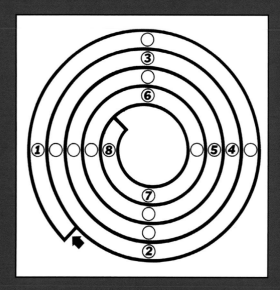

SPIRAL ADDAGE

A sample solution is given here, but others remain. Starting at the arrow, as you travel inward to the center of the spiral, drop off the numbers 1 through 8 consecutively at the circles of your choice. Upon reaching the end of the spiral, each of the four rows of circles must total nine. Find the five remaining solutions.

Solution on page 328.

31.

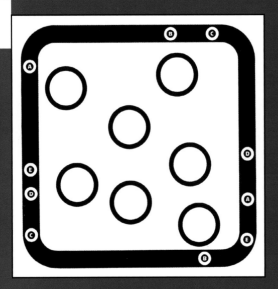

DISC
COUNTS

To begin, draw five straight lines that connect identical letters located on the perimeter of the puzzle (A to A, B to B, etc.). Now, position the numbers 1 through 7 in the seven discs so that each of the five lines totals the same number.

Solution on page 332.

(Need a clue? Turn to page 53.)

$$\boxed{18} \quad \boxed{21} \quad \boxed{3} \quad \boxed{101} \quad \boxed{313} = \boxed{1000}$$

$$\boxed{936} \quad \boxed{504} \quad \boxed{24} \quad \boxed{107} \quad \boxed{8} = \boxed{1000}$$

$$\boxed{550} \quad \boxed{22} \quad \boxed{11} \quad \boxed{5} \quad \boxed{730} = \boxed{1000}$$

GRAND SLAM

Before you are three separate challenges. It is your task to insert the four different mathematical operations (addition, subtraction, multiplication, and division) between the boxes in each equation in such a way that the final outcome is 1,000. You must perform each mathematical operation in the order in which it appears.

Solution on page 325.

Clue to puzzle 26: On the twenty-fourth step, the left foot has finished a cycle. The right foot is three prints short of a cycle. Therefore, a stride of thirty inches has been reached. This means each step taken by the left foot increases the stride by $2^{1}/_{2}$ inches, arrived at by dividing thirty inches by twelve steps.

33.

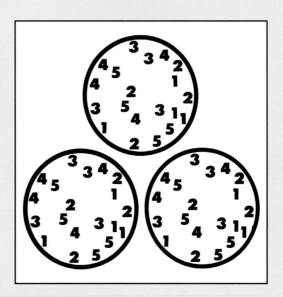

TRIPLE PLAY

Each of these circular playing fields contains an identical arrangement
of numbers. Your challenge is to solve each circle in a different manner.
1) Using two straight lines, divide the first circle into three pieces that
each total twenty. 2) Using two straight lines, divide the next circle into
four pieces that each total fifteen. 3) Using three straight lines, divide the
last circle into five pieces that each total twelve.

Solution on page 320.

34.

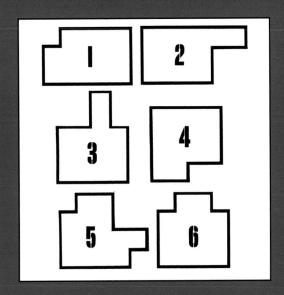

**PAIR
UPS**

Pair up the six shapes in this puzzle to form three pieces of equal size and shape.

Solution on page 322.

35.

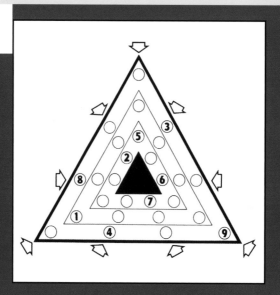

CONCENTRIC
CONCENTRATION

Each of the concentric triangles in this puzzle sports nine circles. As a head start, nine numbers have already been positioned in these circles. Position the missing numbers in the following manner: 1) The numbers 1 through 9 must appear in each triangle. 2) Each side of each triangle (four circles) must total twenty. 3) Each row of three numbers illustrated with arrows must total fifteen.

Solution on page 324.

OPTICAL
DIVERSION

In this puzzle, find the three building blocks that contain the numbers
1 through 9. To reveal your answer, simply black out all unnecessary
parts of the pyramid.

Solution on page 325.

(Need a clue? Turn to page 56.)

37.

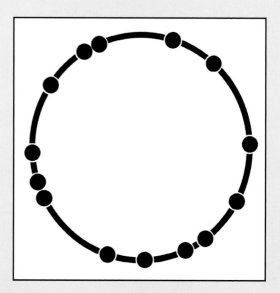

CRISSCROSS CRISIS

Create the largest number of intersections possible (twenty-one) in the interior of this circle by drawing seven straight lines that utilize all fourteen spots on the perimeter. Each line must connect two spots. Here is a second challenge: How many spots are required before ten times this number of intersections are possible? This figure can be calculated without drawing the circle.

Solution on page 328.

38.

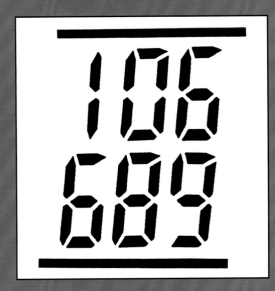

AMPLE TURNOVERS

Carefully examine the two three-digit numbers in this puzzle. When added together they total 795. Now, turn the page upside down and you'll see they now total 1,590—that's exactly twice the original total of 795. Can you find another pair of three-digit numbers that produce this same phenomenon using two new totals? Just as in the example, you may not repeat numbers in a single figure, and your numbers may never begin with a zero.

Solution on page 330.

Clue to puzzle 28: The four totals are eighteen, twenty, twenty-four, and twenty-six.

TRIMMING THE TREE

This Christmas tree has been decorated with a string of thirty-one lights. The color of four bulbs has already been determined. It is known that one of the light sockets is broken. You must determine which socket is broken so that the remaining colored lights can be arranged in the following manner: 1) Use an equal number of red, blue, yellow, orange, and green lights. 2) Position these lights on the string in a repetitive order (example: R-B-Y-O-G, R-B-Y-O-G, etc.). 3) The five lights along both sides of the tree must include all five colors.

Solution on page 332.

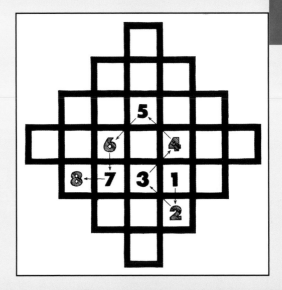

SIDESTEP

Here is a strategic paper-and-pencil game for two players: to win the game, simply create a box canyon that allows you to make the last move. Play begins at any square and continues with players alternating moves to any open adjacent horizontal, vertical, or diagonal square. In the example game above, you are the odd player. It is your move and challenge to set up a box canyon that allows you to win on move eleven.

Solution on page 320.

41.

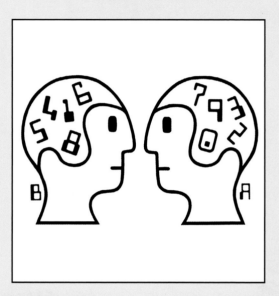

FIGUREHEADS

Figure A has discovered that he can create a five-digit number that is exactly five times greater than a five-digit number that Figure B can create. However, Figure B has discovered that his number can be twice the size of the number Figure A can create by simply eliminating A's zero. What are the numbers that A and B are thinking of?

Solution on page 322

42.

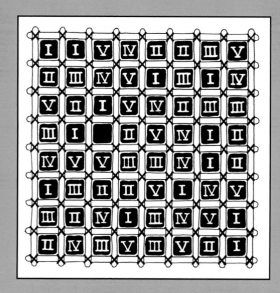

ROMAN STONE GAME

Blacken the surface of twenty-four stones in this puzzle in such a way that the eight horizontal and eight vertical rows will each contain five stones of different numeric value. One stone has already been blackened for you.

Solution on page 324.

43.

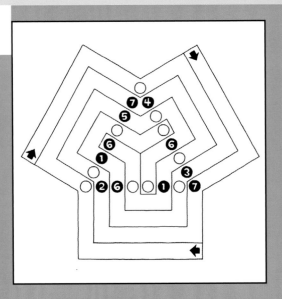

TRAIL 'N' ERROR

Each spiraling trail in this puzzle must contain the numbers 1 through 7. Eleven numbers have already been positioned. Arrange the missing numbers in such a way that each side of the equilateral triangle will total thirty-two.

Solution on page 326.

UP TO SPECS

Position the numbers 1 through 15 on the fifteen unbroken lenses in this puzzle. Do this in such a way that each pair of spectacles totals fifteen and each horizontal, vertical, and diagonal row of four lenses totals thirty.

Solution on page 328.

45.

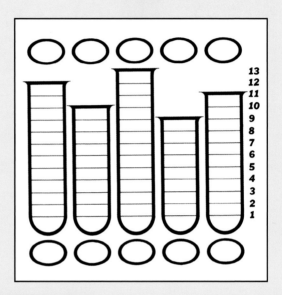

GRADUATE SCHOOL

These five test tubes are graduated in one-ounce increments as marked on the right. The ovals below the tubes are for charting the ounces of water in each. The ovals above are for charting the unfilled ounces of each tube. Your challenge is to fill the five test tubes with a total of twenty-nine ounces of water to fulfill the following criteria: 1) From left to right each test tube must contain more water. 2) The ovals above and below must divulge the numbers 1 through 10.

Solution on page 330

46.

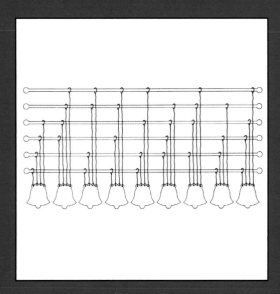

BAR BELLS

Give each of the bells in this puzzle a different number from 1 to 9. If the bells are given the correct numbers, each bar will total exactly thirty. The strings show to which bars the number in each bell must be added.

Solution on page 320.

(Need a clue? Turn to page 64.)

Clue to puzzle 31: Triskaidekaphobes, beware!

47.

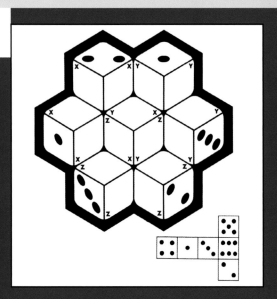

**NEVER
SAY
DIE**

Position the missing pips on the seven standard dice of this puzzle. Do this in such a way that each of the three six-pointed stars that are identified by the letters X, Y, and Z contain all six pip patterns. The illustrated foldout of a standard die must be used in solving the puzzle.

Solution on page 322.

BEHIND CLOSED DOORS

Opening one of the numbered doors shown cancels out two numbers, the number on the door itself and the door covered by the opened door. (For example, opening the first door cancels both the 2 on the door itself and the 6 on the door below, which it covers.) In compensation, behind each door is a number, revealed when the door is opened, that is half the value of the number on the door. Can you open four doors so that all the horizontal and vertical rows add up to the same total?

Solution on page 324.

(Need a clue? Turn to page 65.)

49.

THE OLYMPI-ADD

Place the numbers 1 through 9 in the nine divided areas that make up these Olympic Rings so that the sum of any pair of overlapping rings will total twenty-two. There are two possible solutions.

Solution on page 326

Clue to puzzle 36: Instead of bird's-eye view (from above), the cubes you seek defy gravity to give a worm's-eye view (from below)

50.

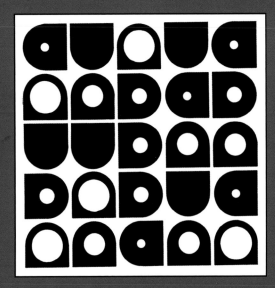

ABSTRACT TREASON

The abstract scheme of this puzzle has been sabotaged by switching the position of two shapes. The original design presented a layout in which the five different-type symbols could all be linked in a repetitive manner (for example, using numbers for shapes, 1-2-3-4-5, 1-2-3-4-5, etc.) with a single continuous line traveling horizontally, vertically, and diagonally from one adjacent shape to another. Your challenge is to restore the original design scheme to the puzzle and trace the path that links all of these shapes.

Solution on page 329.

51.

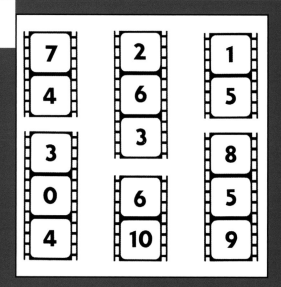

THE SPLICE
IS RIGHT

Splice the six clips of film in this puzzle to produce one fifteen-frame short feature. The final result must be a strip that presents a mathematically logical number sequence.

Solution on page 330.

52.

MAGIC
WORD SQUARES

Each letter in this puzzle represents a different number from 0 to 9. It is your challenge to switch these letters back to numbers in such a way that each horizontal, vertical, and diagonal row of three words totals the same number. Your total for this puzzle is 1,167.

Solution on page 321.

(Need a clue? Turn to page 68.)

53.

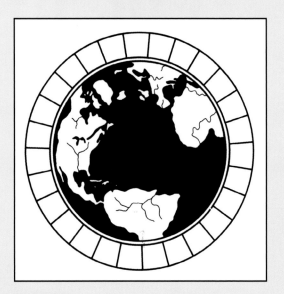

GLOBE TROTTER

You have one year to tour the globe (365 days). During your tour, twenty-seven stops must be made (symbolized by the twenty-seven squares encircling the globe). To complete this tour, you must create a schedule by selecting two numbers that signify both the number of stops you will make and the total number of days that will be spent at each stop. (Example: If one of your numbers is ten, this means that you must make ten stops and spend ten days at each stop for a total of 100 days.) Your task is to find two numbers that create a combined total of twenty-seven stops and use a total of 365 days.

Solution on page 324

54.

ivide this rug into nine pieces of equal size and shape. The design
lement within each shape must be identical.

Solution on page 323.

55.

TACKS
REFORM

A thrifty yet geometrically esthetic carpenter has discovered a way to use only six tacks to secure all nine pieces of wood in such a way that no single piece of wood can slide. He positioned the tacks to create four equilateral triangles. How did he do it?

Solution on page 326.

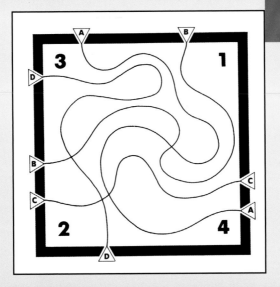

WHIPPER SNAPPER

Four whips (AA, BB, CC, and DD) divide this puzzle into nine irregular shapes. There are six shapes that border each whip. The numbers 1 through 9 must be placed in these shapes to assure that all shapes that border each individual whip will total exactly thirty. The numbers 1 through 4 have been positioned for you.

Solution on page 329.

57.

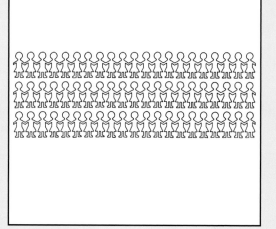

TALLY OF THE DOLLS

For each row of twenty-one paper dolls, select a number and make two cuts dividing the row into three groups so that, by using the number twice in the blanks, you complete (and illustrate) the following mathematical statement:

The tally of the dolls in the left group is _____ times larger than the tally of the dolls in the middle group; the tally of the dolls in the middle group is also _____ times larger than the tally of the dolls in the right group.

Solution on page 332

Clue to puzzle 46: Ring up a 3 on the first be

58.

SIX SHOOTER

There are twenty-six gun sights in this puzzle. With the aid of a compass or piece of string, draw six arcs of equal radius that pass through the crosshairs of each gun sight.

Solution on page 321.

Clue to puzzle 48: Each horizontal and vertical row must total twenty.

59.

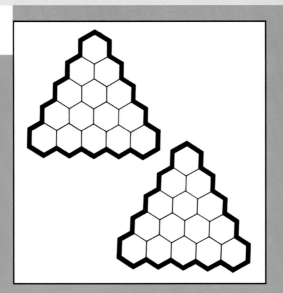

AH
HEX!

There are two ways to solve this problem of topology. Using the fewest
number of colors, color all fifteen hexagons to fulfill the following requirements: 1) No adjacent hexagon may be of the same color. 2) All hexagons
of identical color must be an equal distance apart from one another.

Solution on page 323.

(Need a clue? Turn to page 72.)

V DECEIT

Cut the top triangular figure into three V-shaped pieces that can be reassembled to form the bottom figure, which is shown in reduced scale.

Solution on page 324.

61.

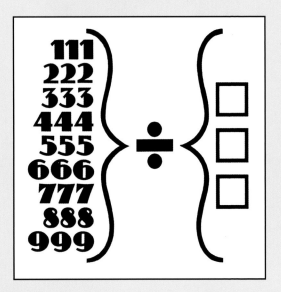

DEVIOUS DIVIDERS

Besides the number 1, can you find three whole numbers that will divide evenly into each of the nine three-digit numbers in this puzzle?

Solution on page 329

Clue to puzzle 52: ORB = 380

62.

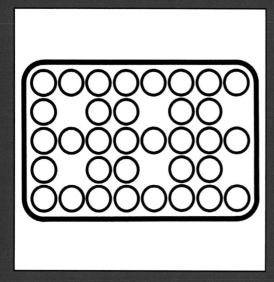

**TAKE
FIVE**

There are thirty-four circles in this puzzle. Your challenge is to remove five circles to leave five.

Solution on page 321.

(Need a clue? Turn to page 74.)

63.

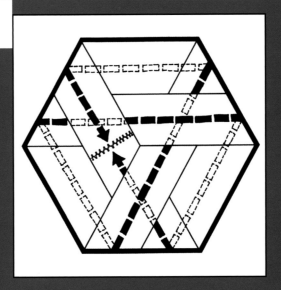

STRIP
PROVOKER

Illustrated in this puzzle is a single strip of paper that has been folded and stitched together at both ends. Find the easiest way to determine the approximate total length of the strip. It is known that the width of this strip is $7/8$ of an inch.

Solution on page 324.

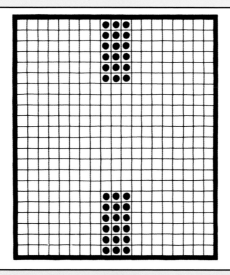

COUNT CADENCE

Eight different commands are necessary to maneuver the eighteen-man drill team in this puzzle from the position below to the position above. It is known that the first command is, "Nine squares forward march." The remaining seven commands are listed in a scrambled manner below:

     Fourteen squares left flank march.

     Ten squares to the rear march.

     Five squares left flank march.

     Six squares right flank march.

     Thirteen squares to the rear march.

     Four squares right flank march.

     Seven squares left flank march.

Solution on page 326.

65.

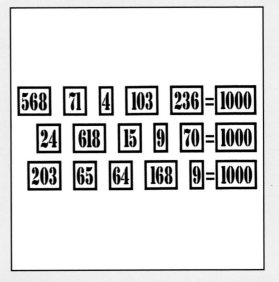

GRAND SLAM

Before you are three separate challenges. It is your task to insert the four different mathematical operations (addition, subtraction, multiplication, and division) between the boxes in each equation in such a way that the final outcome is 1,000. You must perform each mathematical operation in the order in which it appears.

Solution on page 332

Clue to puzzle 59: Each color must form an equilateral triangle

66.

Fig. 1
All lines are equal.
There are at least
three 90° angles.

Fig. 2
Use only two
different lengths
of line.

GEOMETRACTS

Here are two distorted geometric figures. Both have been stretched in such a way that the original figure is unrecognizable at first glance. Your task is to straighten all the lines in each figure to reveal its original identity. The circled letters designate the intersection of two or more lines. Vital clues are given for each figure.

Solution on page 326.

67.

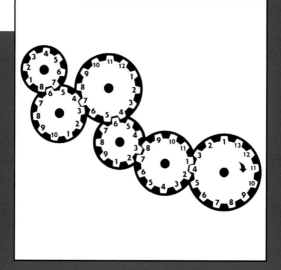

TOOTH
PACE

This puzzle will help you brush up on your mechanical aptitude. Rotate the large gear on the right in the direction of the arrow until the number 3 is in the position now occupied by the number 4. You must then calculate which three teeth will mesh together at each of the five gear junctures.

Solution on page 329.

Clue to puzzle 62: Darkening various circles may literally help you see things more clearly.

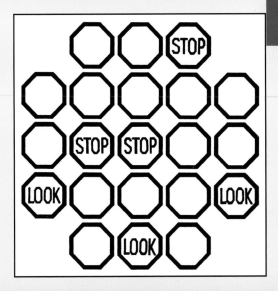

68.

STOP AND LOOK
LESSON

Partition this configuration of twenty-one octagons into three individual pieces that each contain seven octagons. Now, separate the pieces and rearrange them in such a way that the original configuration of octagons is reconstructed, with these exceptions: 1) The stop signs must be adjacent and located in a straight line. 2) The look signs must be adjacent and located in a straight line.

Solution on page 331.

69.

THE MATHEMATICIAN'S FIGURE-EIGHT CAKEWALK

Illustrated here is a thirty-one-square mathematician's cakewalk in the shape of a figure eight. All figure-eight cakewalks are numbered in the following manner: Starting at the center square 0, move one step and label that square "1," move two steps and label that square "2," and so on, proceeding consecutively, until all squares are filled. Continue moving in the same direction and always travel straight through the intersection. Although previously numbered squares may be stepped on more than once, they may never be landed upon again. In the world of mathematics, fewer than twenty such cakewalks can be constructed using the first one million numbers in our number system. See if you can create the next-smaller and the next-larger figure-eight cakewalks.

70.

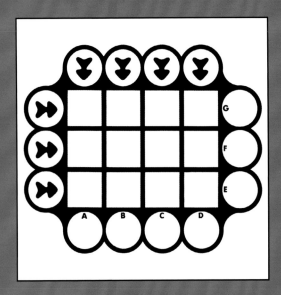

CONSECUTIVE DECISION

Beginning at the letter A, position a series of seven consecutive numbers from lowest to highest in the seven circles. Next, select another series of twelve consecutive numbers and place them in the twelve squares so that the sum of each horizontal and vertical row will total the number in the respective circle.

Solution on page 323.

(Need a clue? Turn to page 79.)

SUNSTROKE

Fill in the six numbers that are missing from the empty sunspots. To get you started in the right "direction," three sunspot totals have been positioned for you. All thirty-six of the satellite numbers that hover around the sunspots determine the nine sunspot totals.

Solution on page 327.

RING AROUND THE ROSES

There are fifteen roses in this puzzle. It is your challenge to draw four circles that will enclose an odd number of roses. Also, each circle must enclose a different number of roses. No circle may touch or intersect another circle.

Solution on page 327.

Clue to puzzle 70: Nine is A good place to start.

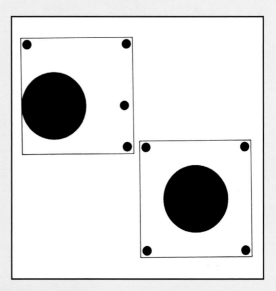

THE CARPENTER &
THE GLASS CUTTER

In this puzzle you must determine the best solution for two craftsmen;
one is working with wood and the other is working with glass. Using the
fewest straight cuts per craftsman, cut the top square figure into the
fewest number of pieces that can be rearranged to form the bottom
square figure. The white area is transparent for the glass cutter.

Solution on page 33

74.

~TAR OF DIVIDE

~ing only four straight lines, divide this six-pointed star into four
~ctions, each containing one of the mathematical symbols. Create these
~isions in such a way that, when the mathematical symbol is performed
~h the number 3 and the number of triangles in that section, all of the
~swers will be the same. In other words, add 3 to the number
~triangles within the addition segment, subtract 3 from the number of
~angles in the subtraction segment, multiply by 3 the number of triangles
~the multiplication segment, and divide 3 into the number of triangles in
~e division segment to achieve the same number.

Solution on page 331.

2

Test Your PUZZLE IQ

1.

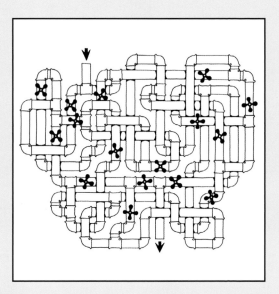

WATER
GATES

Open the fewest number of valves that will allow water to flow from one arrow to the other. Play begins with all valves in the closed position.

Solution on page 334

[Need a clue? Turn to page 86]

2.

BARREL
OF LAPS

Complete two closed laps around the barrels in this puzzle in such a way that A encircles twice as many barrels and twice as many points as B. Several low-scoring solutions exist. It is your task to encircle the highest number of barrels and points for lap A.

Solution on page 335.

(Need a clue? Turn to page 89.)

3.

DASH HOUNDS

Seven dachshunds competing in the 100-yard dash wear seven numbers from 1 to 7. It is your task to insert these seven numbers in the following seven equations to determine how each of the seven dachshunds finished the race.

1st place	+	4th place	=	2nd place	+	5th place
4th place	+	6th place	=	1st place	+	5th place
1st place	+	2nd place	=	5th place	+	6th place
2nd place	+	6th place	=	3rd place	+	5th place
2nd place	+	3rd place	=	1st place	+	6th place
1st place	+	3rd place	=	2nd place	+	7th place
3rd place	+	6th place	=	1st place	+	7th place

Solution on page 337.

Clue to puzzle 1: Open three valves.

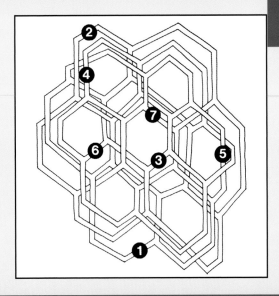

HONEYCOMB
HEXAGONS

Start at number 1 and trace a path consecutively to each number and then return to number 1. At no time may any passage be used more than once.

Solution on page 339.

5.

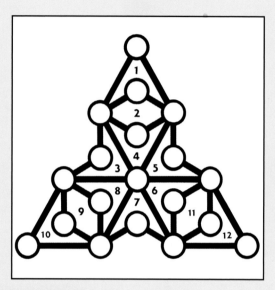

NUMBER NUMBER

Using only the numbers 1 through 4, arrange them in the nineteen circles of this puzzle to fulfill the following conditions: 1) The corners of the twelve identified four-sided shapes must each contain the numbers 1, 2, 3, and 4. 2) The perimeter of the six-pointed star (made up of pieces 3, 4, 5, 6, 7, and 8) in the center of the puzzle must total the lowest possible score.

Solution on page 34

(Need a clue? Turn to page 91

6.

ITTING DUCKS

here are three different kinds of ducks in this puzzle. Position six more ucks on this two-dimensional pond so that each of the five horizontal and ertical rows will sport all three different kinds of sitting ducks.

Solution on page 343.

Clue to puzzle 2: Lap A will completely encircle B.

7.

C SICK

Travel through this maze connecting each of the seven dots with one continuous meandering line. No passageway or intersection may be used more than once. Your starting and finishing points are located in the dead-end passageways.

Solution on page 338.

RR XING

Trace two paths on this maze of overlapping and intersecting roadways. Each path must be a closed loop that encircles two identical Rs. At no time may any path be traveled more than once.

Solution on page 335.

Clue to puzzle 5: Place the number 4 in the center circle.

9.

CANDY COUNTER

From the following clues, determine how much candy is in each jar: 1) In all there are 221 pieces of candy. 2) The number of jelly beans is equal to one-third of the gum balls. 3) The number of peppermints is equal to one-third of the jelly beans. 4) The number of red-hots is equal to one-third of the gum balls and jelly beans.

Solution on page 342

(Need a clue? Turn to page 95

10.

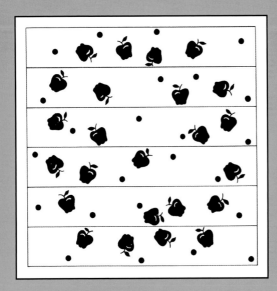

PINE APPLES

Connect five knotholes with five straight lines to create six divisions that contain one apple each. One apple from each plank must be utilized in constructing this solution.

Solution on page 338.

Need a clue? Turn to page 97.

11.

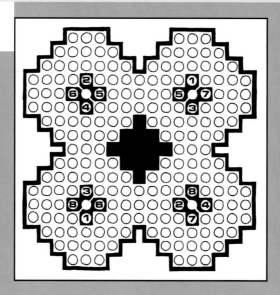

CROSS LINKS

Using the fewest number of circles, construct eight individual chains
from 1 to 1, 2 to 2, etc. Each chain may travel horizontally, vertically,
and diagonally to any unused adjacent circle. Chains may never crisscross.
Note: Each home base of four numbers allows for one diagonal passage
through its center circle.

Solution on page 340.

THE FRENCH CONNECTION

Trace two paths through this French labyrinth using the same seven-word
yes/no conversation sequence. One path must travel from A to B, and the
other path must travel from X to Y. Your routes may share the same passages and words.

Solution on page 344.

**Clue to puzzle 9: There are sixty-five
more gum balls than red-hots.**

13.

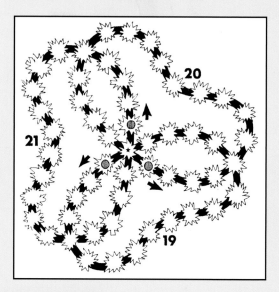

THE INTERCROSSING

Illustrated here are three crisscrossing paths, each containing a designated different number of spaces. Your task is to determine how many moves it will take until all three shaded markers will rendezvous on the center intercrossing identified with a star. All markers will begin moving one step at a time in unison around their individual wreathlike paths in a counterclockwise direction.

Solution on page 334

14.

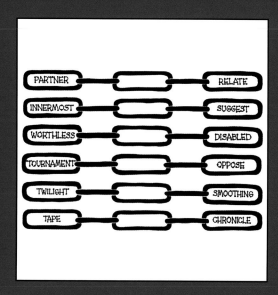

ords that have more than one pronunciation are called homographs.
s your challenge to insert a homograph into each of the vacant links in
s puzzle. Clues to each pronunciation of the missing links are given in
outer links of each individual puzzle chain.

Solution on page 336.

**Clue to puzzle 10: The five straight
lines create a five-pointed star.**

CLOUD NINE

Give each of the blank clouds in this puzzle a different number from 1 to 8.
Do this in such a way that, if you begin at cloud 9, you can total exactly
nine points by drifting along each wind current. Cloud 9 is not tallied in the
total of each current.

Solution on page 346.

(Need a clue? Turn to page 100.)

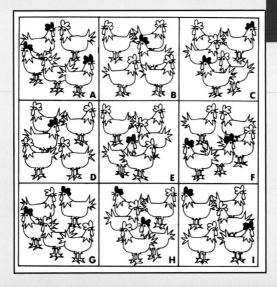

FLY
THE COOP

A disturbance will provoke some of the chickens in coops C, E, G, and I to fly their coops and land in the remaining five coops. When the dust settles there will be a different number of chickens in each coop, and each square of four coops (for example: ABDE) will contain twenty-one chickens, not twenty chickens as presently shown in each such group. Can you create this fowl-play puzzler?

Solution on page 338.

(Need a clue? Turn to page 101.)

17.

POINT BLANKS

Using the numbers 1 through 5 three times each, place one number in each of the fifteen arrowheads to fulfill the following requirements: 1) Ea set of three converging arrowheads must total nine points. 2) Each set two back-to-back arrowheads must total six points.

Solution on page 34

Clue to puzzle 15: Place the number 8 in the top clou

18.

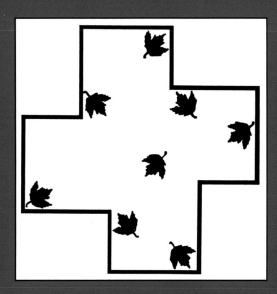

"LEAVES

...vide this figure into eight pieces of equal size and shape in such a way ...at each piece contains one leaf.

Solution on page 339.

(Need a clue? Turn to page 106.)

Clue to puzzle 16: Coop A will contain five chickens.

19.

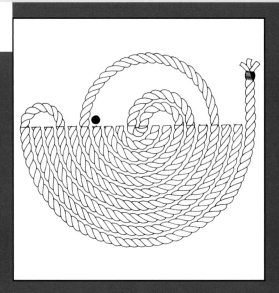

STRANDED

"Stranded" is a stimulating strategy game for two players who begin at the whipped rope end on the far right and continue to connect the running end of the rope, creating one swirling length of rope. Each move consists of drawing in one upper loop that connects to an unused rope section below. Players move alternately, attempting to strand their opponent in a position where he or she cannot make a connection without crossing over a previously positioned rope segment.

Illustrated above is a sample game in progress. Your challenge is to pick up the game at the black dot, making a single move that will guarantee a win in the fewest possible moves. To begin a new game, place a blank sheet of paper over the upper loops and use a pencil to draw in your connections.

Solution on page 343.

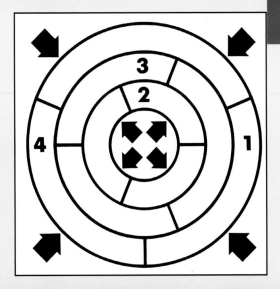

WHAT'S THE POINT?

Place the numbers remaining from the series 1 through 9 in the five vacant divisions of this puzzle. Do this in such a way that the totals of the numbers between each pair of facing arrows will all reveal the identical and highest possible score.

Solution on page 345.

(Need a clue? Turn to page 105.)

FIRE STOPPERS

Travel through this maze and extinguish this ball of flames by using all six
of the fire stoppers. Begin and finish this task on the two dots at the base
of the flames. Completing your mission requires that no passage be used
more than once.

Solution on page 33

22.

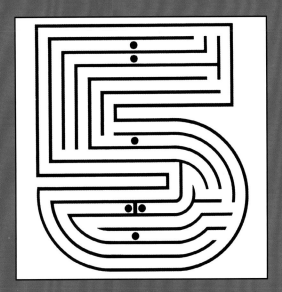

ravel through this maze connecting each of the six dots with one
ontinuous meandering line. No passageway or intersection may be used
nore than once. Your starting and finishing points are located in the
ead-end passageways.

Solution on page 336.

Clue to puzzle 20: The highest possible score is seventeen.

23.

PHONY NUMBERS

Here is a coded word game in which the telephone is instrumental in converting numbers to letters. As seen on a touch-tone or dial phone, each of the numbers used in this puzzle can represent one of three different letters. It is your challenge to convert each line of numbers at right into a word that is related to its puzzle category. It takes one smooth operator to answer the call for each line of phony numbers in this collection of three categories.

Solution on page 338.

Clue to puzzle 18: In case you haven't guessed, the divisions are T–shaped.

MONEY TALK

A•36844
B•27323
C•473362225
D•7326887
E•926786

NATIONAL PARKS

A•96736483
B•3837452337
C•7436263624
D•4522437
E•93556978663

DIG IT

A•384688
B•873624
C•22625
D•9355
E•3694653

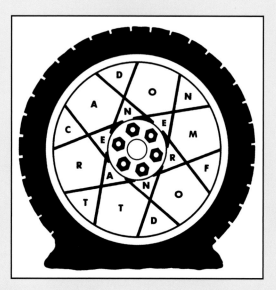

SPOKEN WORDS

This puzzle challenges you to trace the spoken words of the motorist who just received this flat tire. It's just a coincidence, but the motorist's words are the same as those used by the Culpeper Minutemen of the American Revolution. Begin at any letter and trace this phrase from one adjacent unused letter to another. It's not necessary to use all eighteen letters.

Solution on page 34●

(Need a clue? Turn to page 110●

25.

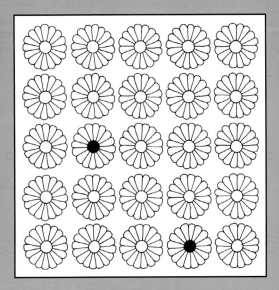

LOWER PLOWER

Without lifting your pencil from the paper, plow through the center of every flower with only eight straight continuous lines. Start and finish at the black-eyed flowers.

Solution on page 344.

TANKS A LOT

A tank force commander must position all of his tanks in a rectangular formation of columns and rows to fulfill the following strategic order: "If all of the tanks on the perimeter of the formation are called into action, there will be exactly twice as many tanks left in reserve as sent into action." If this commander has the minimum number of tanks to carry out such an order, what is this number and how must the tanks be positioned?

Solution on page 342.

(Need a clue? See page 111.)

Clue to puzzle 24: Start by finding a prohibitive contraction.

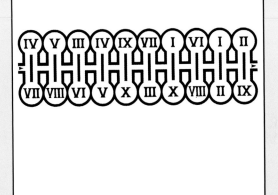

ROAMING NUMBER ROWS

Enter from the left and exit on the right connecting a string of ten different Roman numerals from 1 to 10. At no time may any passage or cul-de-sac be traveled more than once. There are four possible solutions.

Solution on page 346.

Clue to puzzle 26: There are more than 100 tanks.

28.

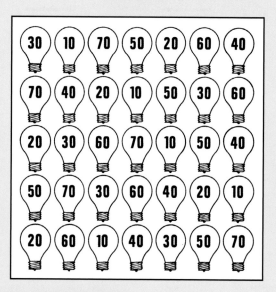

THE LIGHT HEAVYWEIGHT

Knock out fifteen bulbs in such a way that each vertical row totals 100 watts and each horizontal row totals 140 watts.

Solution on page 33

29.

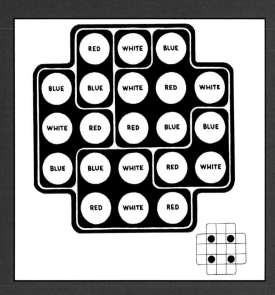

ATRIOTIC SQUARES

arrange the six puzzle pieces to form three different solutions. To solve,
eate a square (illustrated above right) having all red, all white, and
stly, all blue corners.

Solution on page 336.

30.

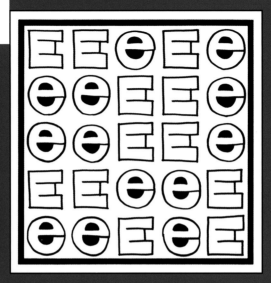

RED E OR NOT

The object of this puzzle is simply to color ten of the twenty-five letters in the puzzle red. However, the following rules must be observed: 1) Each vertical row must contain two red letters that are not adjacent. 2) One letter must be a capital E and the other a lowercase e.

Solution on page 339.

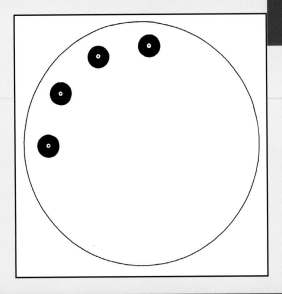

FINE CUT

With two arcs of a compass, divide this circle into three pieces that can be reassembled to form a new circle in which the four disks lie in a straight line.

Solution on page 341.

32.

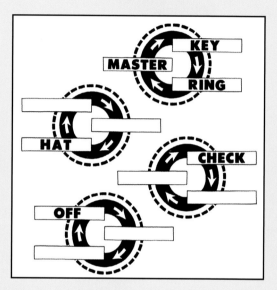

RECYCLE

Here are three separate challenges in which each of the given words mu~~s~~
be recycled. Each word on the recycle wheel must complete the thought
the word it follows. In the example, we have MASTER KEY, KEY RING, ar~~d~~
RINGMASTER.

Upon solving this trio of puzzles, see if you can create your own recyc~~le~~
beginning with a word of your choice.

Solution on page 34▮

33.

OTAL CONFUSION

ravel from A to B scoring the lowest possible score. The passages
mposing the puzzle cross over and under one another and intersect only
the circles.

Solution on page 334.

(Need a clue? Turn to page 118.)

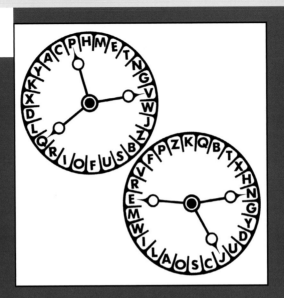

DIAL A PAIR

All twenty-six letters of the alphabet appear on both of these dials. It is your task to rotate the two three-handed pointers in such a way that they both point to the same three letters.

Solution on page 344.

Clue to puzzle 33: The lowest possible total is five.

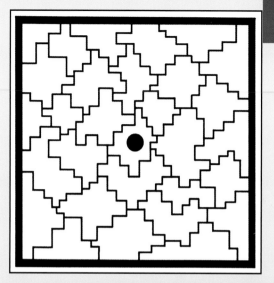

STAIR CRAZY

In this maze of stairways, your task is to step out the shortest route around the center pivot point. Start your climb from any side of the square, but the side from which you begin is the side on which you must finish. Keep track of your route by counting each horizontal and vertical move. No step may be used more than once.

Solution on page 336.

(Need a clue? Turn to page 121.)

35.

36.

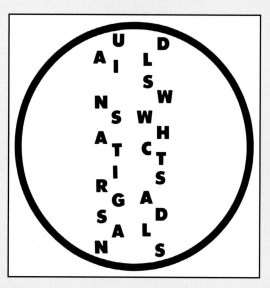

DIVIDE AND CONJURE

Use two straight lines to divide this circular playing field into three sections. If the lines are drawn correctly, the letters within each section can be unscrambled to reveal three related words.

Solution on page 340

(Need a clue? Turn to page 123

37.

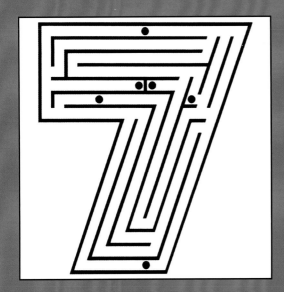

UPSET

...avel through this maze connecting each of the six dots with one ...ntinuous meandering line. No passageway or intersection may be ...ed more than once. Your starting and finishing points are located in ... dead-end passageways.

Solution on page 338.

Clue to puzzle 35: The shortest path requires forty-nine steps.

38.

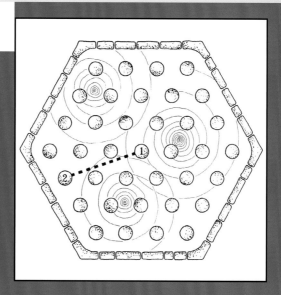

TALL JOHN

Similar to a knight's move in chess, Tall John may only take steps equidistant to his illustrated first step from stone 1 to stone 2 (the long diagonal of a two-by-three parallelogram of six stones). Your task is to continue Tall John on a journey that will take him to every stepping-stone in the pond and return him to the center stone. Stones may not be stepped on more than once, with the sole exception of completing the tour at the center stone.

Solution on page 342.

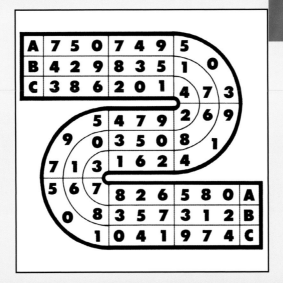

DEAD HEAT

This S-shaped track is divided into nine sections, each having three lettered-lane divisions, A, B, and C. It is your challenge to blacken five whole sections in such a way that the remaining four sections will reveal the numbers 0 through 9 in each of the lane divisions.

Solution on page 344.

Clue to puzzle 36: The words in this puzzle are very timely.

40.

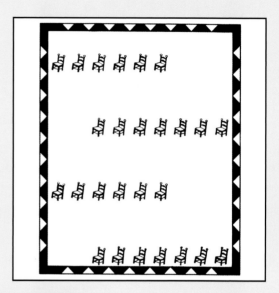

INFERIOR DESIGN

Divide this rectangular room into nine square rooms that will each contain at least one chair. The graduated border will aid you in construct ing the walls.

Solution on page 33

(Need a clue? Turn to page 129

41.

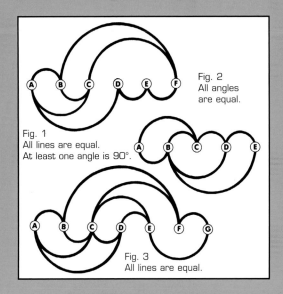

Fig. 2
All angles
are equal.

Fig. 1
All lines are equal.
At least one angle is 90°.

Fig. 3
All lines are equal.

~~G~~EOMETRACTS

~~He~~re are three distorted geometric figures. Each has been stretched in
~~su~~ch a way that the original figure is unrecognizable at first glance. Your
~~ta~~sk is to straighten all the lines in each figure to reveal its original
~~ide~~ntity. The circled letters designate the intersection of two or more
~~lin~~es. Vital clues are given for each figure.

Solution on page 337.

42.

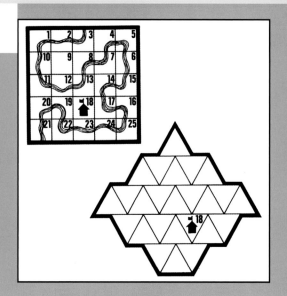

THE OLD RIVER SCHOOL HOUSE

For this topographical puzzle, squares have been distorted into the shape of triangles. Your challenge is to transfer the course of the river from the square grid map on the left to the triangular grid map. As a starter, the schoolhouse has been correctly transferred.

Solution on page 339.

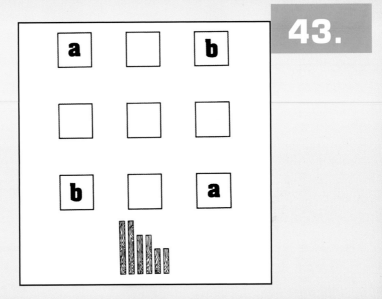

43.

WALKIN' THE PLANKS

Shown here are nine islands, each measuring ten feet square. The horizontal and vertical distances between islands also measure ten feet. Using only the six planks illustrated above, which measure fifteen feet, eleven feet, and seven feet long respectively, how is it possible to construct two catwalks of three planks each from a to a and b to b?

Solution on page 340.

44.

A	A	N	N
B	B	O	O
C	C	P	P
D	D	Q	Q
E	E	R	R
F	F	S	S
G	G	T	T
H	H	U	U
I	I	V	V
J	J	W	W
K	K	X	X
L	L	Y	Y
M	M	Z	Z

WORDMASTER

Here's a vocabulary quiz that challenges you to fill in as many of the twenty-six blanks as possible with words that begin and end with the same letter. The longer your words, the higher your score. Any total score of 200 letters or more is considered excellent. Compete with an opponent or try to beat our score. All common words are fair game, including proper nouns, slang, and foreign words.

Solution on page 34

(Need a clue? Turn to page 13

45.

...vel through this maze connecting each of the seven dots with one ...ntinuous meandering line. No passageway or intersection may be used ...re than once. Your starting and finishing points are located in the dead-...d passageways.

Solution on page 344.

Clue to puzzle 40: All rooms need not be of the same size.

DUELING
THREADS

Using straight lines only, thread all the needles in this puzzle with two threads. One thread must link the black needles, and the other thread must link the white needles. Threads may never cross over needles or other threads. Begin at the two needles marked A and B.

Solution on page 337.

THE
ASTER RISK

Solve this puzzle by positioning all asterisks of identical number in straight lines. You must accomplish this feat by removing the fewest number of asterisks and then repositioning them in the original locations of the removed asterisks. At present, only the number 4 asterisks are in a straight line. Lines may be horizontal, vertical, or diagonal, and asterisks need not be adjacent.

Solution on page 339.

(Need a clue? Turn to page 134.)

48.

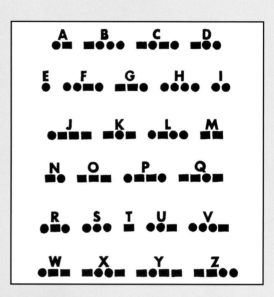

MORSE DECODER

The international Morse code (above) consists of dots, dashes, and spaces. However, for this puzzle an interesting problem has been create by the elimination of all spaces. Presented at right are three separate challenges of five words each. It is your task to properly space each numbered row to reveal a word from the given category. Dots and dash are always in the correct order.

Solution on page 3

IT'S GREEN

1. ☐☐○☐○☐○○○
2. ○○○☐○☐○○○☐○○○
3. ☐○○○☐☐○☐○○☐○○
4. ○○☐○☐○○☐○○○☐○○○
5. ○○☐○☐○☐○○○○

FRUIT

1. ☐☐○○☐○○☐○☐○○ .
2. ○☐○☐☐○○☐☐○○☐○○○
3. ☐○○○○☐○○☐○○☐
4. ○☐○○○☐☐☐☐☐○
5. ☐○☐☐○☐☐○○○☐○○○☐○○

PLANETS

1. ☐☐☐☐☐☐○○☐○☐☐
2. ☐☐○○☐○○☐○○○○○
3. ○☐☐☐○☐○○○
4. ○☐☐☐○○☐○○☐○☐○○☐○
5. ☐○☐○○☐☐○☐○☐○○○☐○○○

Clue to puzzle 44: Our S-S word makes "straightforwardness" look short. 279 is our total letter count.

49.

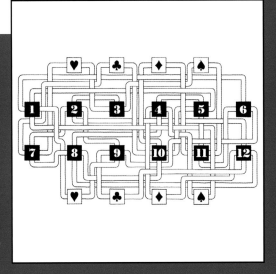

FOUR
PAIR

Trace four separate paths in this puzzle that connect identical card suits. At no time may any passageway or numbered intersection be used more than once. Each path will pass through three numbered squares.

Solution on page 343.

**Clue to puzzle 47: Six asterisks must be
relocated, including one of the 4s.**

ROMAN
STONE GAME

Blacken the surface of twenty-four stones in this puzzle in such a way that the eight horizontal and eight vertical rows will each contain five stones of different numeric value. One stone has already been blackened for you.

Solution on page 341.

51.

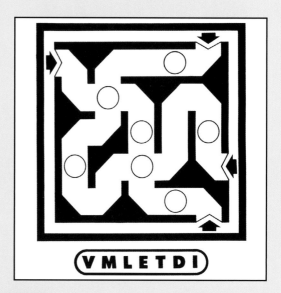

FOURWORDS
BACKWORDS

Transfer the letters given above into the circles on this mazelike pattern of pathways to create four common words that can be read by following the arrows. Always travel straight through the intersections in tracing these words.

Solution on page 34

52.

avel through this maze connecting each of the six dots with one
ntinuous meandering line. No passageway or intersection may be
sed more than once. Your starting and finishing points are located in
e dead-end passageways.

Solution on page 346.

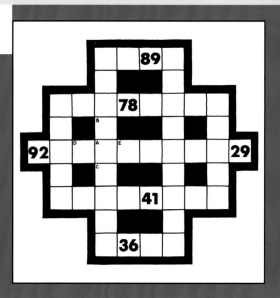

DOUBLE-UP

Assign a number to every empty square in this puzzle to fulfill the following condition: Any square located between two adjacent horizontal or vertical squares must be exactly half the total of the two squares. For example, if the number 25 is placed in square A, then squares B and C must total fifty, and D and E must also total fifty. Six numbers have already been positioned.

Solution on page 337.

(Need a clue? Turn to page 140.)

TICKY
TACKY

Trace a path from A to B connecting each of the pushpins with one continuous line. At no time may any passage be used more than once.

Solution on page 339.

55.

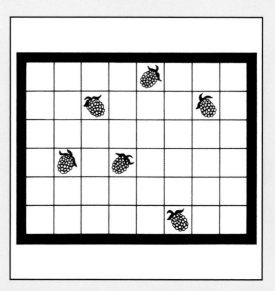

BERRY
INTERESTING

Here's a puzzle in which the squares you don't use are just as important as the squares you do use. Connect all six berries in this puzzle with a continuous line that travels horizontally and vertically through exactly half of the squares on the board. The unused squares must produce a path of squares that is the mirror image of the berry path.

Solution on page 34

**Clue to puzzle 53: Position the numbe
85 adjacent to 92 on the gri**

56.

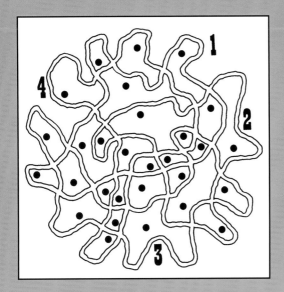

GH TRAIL IT

ere are four numbered hiking trails in this puzzle. Each trail is a continu-
s loop and crisscrosses the other trails. Individual trails can be traced by
ways traveling straight through intersections without making left or right
rns. Knowing that the illustrated dots represent campgrounds, solve the
llowing problems: 1) Which is the only campground surrounded by all
ur trails? 2) Which two trails overlap and share the most surrounded
mpgrounds? 3) Which three trails overlap and share the most
rrounded campgrounds?

Solution on page 341.

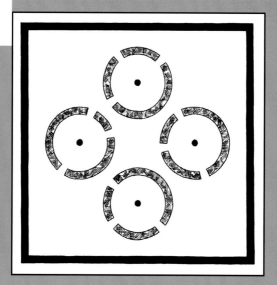

THE ENTERING DILEMMA

Using only five straight lines, travel through the most favorable openings of the rings and link together all four center spots. All lines must remain within the square boundary.

Solution on page 346.

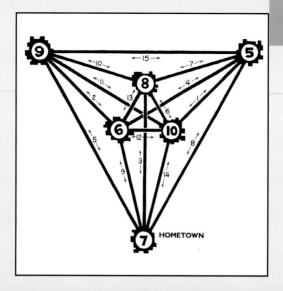

ROUND TRIP DECISION

Here is your challenge. Start at Hometown with seven dollars and begin a round trip visiting each city and then returning home with exactly zero cash. Through your trip you must pay in advance the designated dollar tolls along each selected route of travel. Upon reaching each city you will receive the posted dollar figure to add to your travel money.

Solution on page 335.

(Need a clue? Turn to page 145.)

59.

O	I	N	O	P	S	A	U	T	A
N	C	A	R	A	A	Y	R	O	B
U	A	G	E	R	M	A	R	K	A
L	S	U	W	I	N	R	U	T	G
I	F	L	O	P	M	U	C	S	A
S	H	N	I	P	S	S	A	S	E
I	C	A	D	R	A	T	R	R	R
D	H	R	G	C	C	O	R	O	C
A	R	E	L	O	R	N	B	T	R
S	N	E	I	C	O	W	A	T	E

TANGLE WORD

Using all 100 letters in this puzzle, reveal the related words and discover
the mystery category. The words may be spelled out horizontally and
vertically, forward or backward, many with twists and turns, but never
scrambled. One word has been outlined to give you a start; partitioning
off the rest is up to you. Letters may be used only once.

Solution on page 33

60.

CRYPTIC CALENDAR

...ing four straight lines that touch the center spot, divide this calendar ...o seven divisions that will each spell a different day of the week. The ...ers within any division may be scrambled.

Solution on page 346.

Clue to puzzle 58: Begin by paying the five-dollar toll.

61.

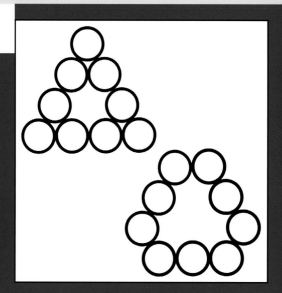

COINFUSION

To solve this puzzle you'll need nine coins or circular objects of equal size. First, arrange these coins in the shape of the pyramid at left. Then, by sliding one coin at a time, construct the figure at right in the least possible number of moves. Each moved coin must always come to rest touching at least two other coins.

Solution on page 345.

(Need a clue? Turn to page 150.)

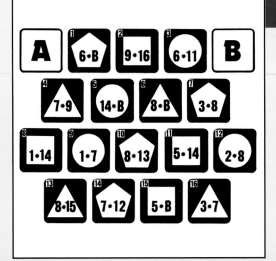

SHAPE AHOY

Each of the destination squares in this puzzle is numbered from 1 through 16 (upper left-hand corners) and displays one of four geometric shapes. It is your challenge to travel from A to B by way of four destination squares that contain a circle, square, triangle, and pentagon, not necessarily in that order. The numbers and letters appearing within the geometric shapes tell you which destination squares you may elect to advance to next. From A, you may advance to any destination square.

Solution on page 343.

(Need a clue? Turn to page 151.)

63.

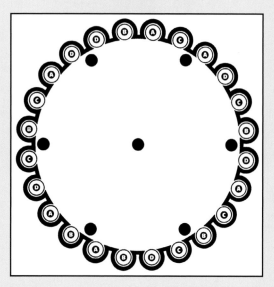

RINKY LINKS

Select six of the same-lettered circles around the perimeter and draw three straight lines linking pairs of the circles to divide the rink into seve sections. Each section must contain only one black spot.

Solution on page 33

(Need a clue? Turn to page 15

64.

SISSIMA PARADOX

Hidden in the above grid are rows made up of the same set of scrambled letters. These rows may be both horizontal, both vertical, or one of each. Can you find them?

Solution on page 337.

(Need a clue? Turn to page 155.)

65.

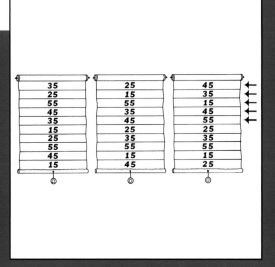

35	25	45	←
25	15	35	←
55	55	15	←
45	35	45	←
35	45	55	←
15	25	25	
25	35	35	
55	55	55	
45	15	15	
15	45	25	

105
IN THE SHADES

Partially raise one or more of the shades in this puzzle until the top five horizontal rows of numbers total 105 apiece.

Solution on page 340.

(Need a clue? Turn to page 156.)

Clue to puzzle 61: Four moves are required.

FLYING COLORS

Four colors appear on the eight flags in this puzzle (R = red, B = blue, G = green, Y = yellow). Rearrange only three flags in such a way that no identical color can be seen in any of the eight illustrated horizontal or vertical rows. Flags may not be turned upside down.

Solution on page 341.

Clue to puzzle 62: From A, first travel to square number 10.

67.

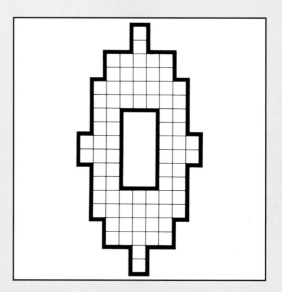

NIDDY GRIDDY

Divide this figure into eight pieces of equal size and shape.

Solution on page 34

Clue to puzzle 63: It's a matter of C-ing correct

68.

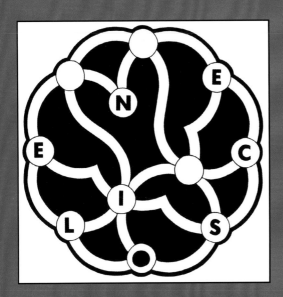

TONGUE TWISTER

This puzzle consists of two separate challenges: 1) See how many different words you can find that contain all the letters in the puzzle. 2) See how many of these words you can trace with one continuous line, starting at the black spot. No passage or intersection may be used more than once per word.

Solution on page 338.

69.

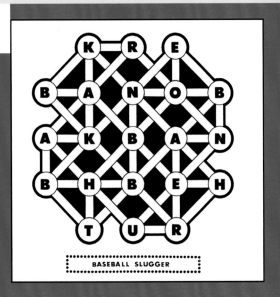

BASEBALL SLUGGER

PEOPLE PUZZLE

Hidden in this crisscrossing network of passageways is the first and last name of a well-known person. A clue to the identity is given in the box above. Select a starting letter and trace this name with a continuous line. At no time may any letter or passage be reused.

Solution on page 336.

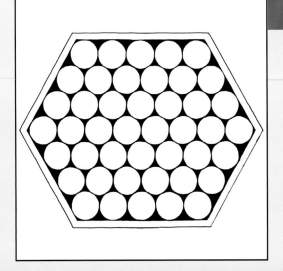

DISC JOCKEY

Shown here is a rack of forty-four disks creating a hexagon having sides comprising 4, 4, 5, 4, 4, and 5 disks. Can you create another forty-four-disk hexagon having sides of 2, 3, 4, 5, 6, and 7 disks, not necessarily in that order?

Solution on page 345.

Clue to puzzle 64: Both rows are vertical.

71.

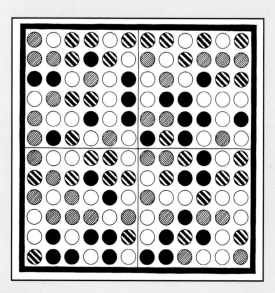

REVERSE
GERRYMANDER

This puzzle is presently divided into four districts in which the white spot[s] outnumber any other color in each district. It is your mission to redraw the lines to form four new districts of equal size and shape so that each [of] the four colors has a majority in one district.

Solution on page 34[?]

Clue to puzzle 65: Raise the middle shade four row[s]

72.

HE MATHEMATICIAN'S CAKEWALK

strated here is a thirty-two-square mathematician's cakewalk. All
athematician's cakewalks are numbered in the following manner:
arting at square 0, move clockwise one step and label that square "1."
ove two steps and label that square "2," and so on, consecutively, until
squares are filled. Although previously numbered squares may be
epped on more than once, they may never be landed upon again. In the
rld of mathematics, fewer than twenty such cakewalks can be construct-
using the first one million numbers in our number system. See if you
n create the next smaller and the next larger cakewalks.

Solution on page 345.

3

Mystifying
MATH
PUZZLES

1.

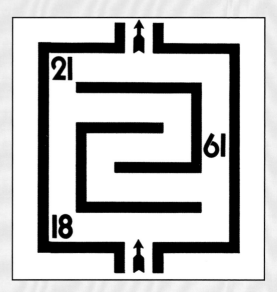

THE WORLD'S EASIEST MAZE

Travel through this maze totaling exactly 100 points. No passage or intersection may be used more than once. Enter and exit the maze at the designated arrows.

Solution on page 34

2.

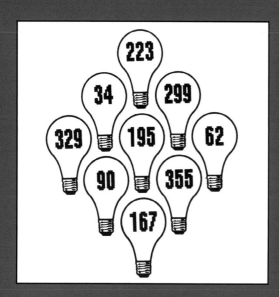

WATTS WRONG?

Three light bulbs in this puzzle have been incorrectly numbered by plus or minus one. It is your challenge to determine which bulbs need to be changed and correct their numbers to create a magic square in which the horizontal row, vertical row, and all six diagonal rows of three bulbs total the same number.

Solution on page 350.

(Need a clue? Turn to page 164.)

3.

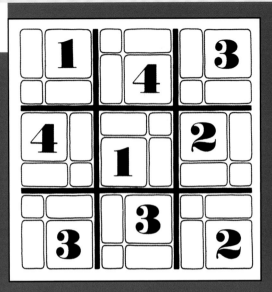

POSITIVE PLACEMENT

The nine numbered blocks in this puzzle predetermine the numeric value
of all twenty-seven remaining blocks. Solve as follows: 1) Each subdivision
of four blocks must reveal the numbers 1, 2, 3, and 4. 2) Adjacent blocks
(horizontally or vertically) may never be of identical numeric value, even if
they are in different subdivisions.

Solution on page 352.

OAKIE
DOKIE

The age of three grand oaks totals exactly 1,000 years. From the following information, determine the age of each tree: When the youngest tree has reached the age of the middle tree, the middle tree will be the age of the oldest tree and four times the current age of the youngest tree.

Solution on page 354.

5.

FLOATING HEDGES 1

Draw a continuous line through this maze, connecting the numbers 1 through 7 consecutively. You may not travel the same passageway more than once.

Solution on page 35

Clue to puzzle 2: Each row totals 58

6.

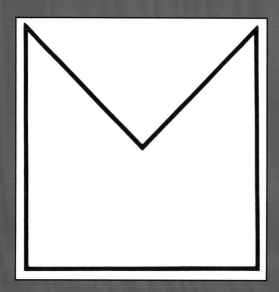

BE WARNED

Things are not always what they appear to be. This may be the easiest dissection puzzle you'll ever tackle. It all depends on how you approach the problem. Two fathers and two sons wish to divide this irregular-shaped parcel of land evenly among themselves. Each parcel must be identical in size and shape. How can this be done?

Solution on page 358.

7.

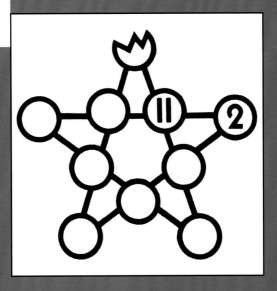

BROKEN PENTAGRAM

It's possible to position ten consecutive numbers on an unbroken pentagram of ten circles in such a way that each straight line of four circles totals exactly the same number. Here we issue the same challenge but with a little twist. Of ten consecutive numbers, place nine in the nine unbroken circles in such a way that each straight line of three or four unbroken circles totals exactly twenty-four. Two numbers have been positioned for you.

Solution on page 361.

(Need a clue? Turn to page 168.)

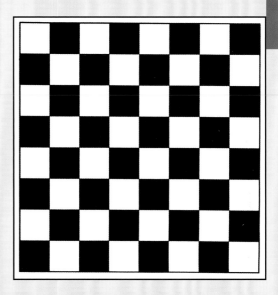

SQUARE SHOOTER

A standard checkerboard measures eight squares by eight squares and contains thirty-two black squares and thirty-two red squares. Exactly 139 other-size checkerboards, ranging from two by two to seven by seven squares, exist on a standard checkerboard. How many of these smaller-size checkerboards can be found that also contain an equal number of red and black squares?

Solution on page 348.

9.

PRIME BEEF

Here's a magic-square puzzle in which the unbranded eight heads of beef must be branded with a prime number (numbers that can only be divided evenly by one and itself) in such a way that each horizontal, vertical, and diagonal row of three cows totals 111. The lowest and only nonprime number brand (1: an even more elite digit) in the puzzle has been placed to give you a head start.

Solution on page 35

Clue to puzzle 7: Throw out the number

10.

TOTAL CONFUSION

Travel from A to B scoring the lowest possible score. The passages composing the puzzle cross over and under one another and intersect only at the circles.

Solution on page 352.

(Need a clue? Turn to page 171.)

LOVE BUGS

All of the love bugs in this puzzle are sporting from one to six spots on their backs. Your task is to mate six pairs of these love bugs by drawing straight lines that connect two bugs sporting the same number of spots. Further, the six pairs to be mated must include love bugs from each spotted denomination (one through six). At no time may lines or bugs be crossed over in solving this puzzle.

Solution on page 354.

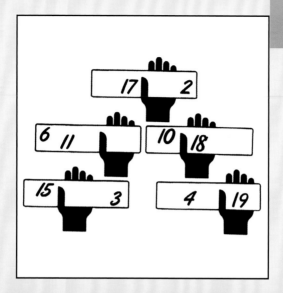

FIVE CARD DRAW

To solve this puzzle, place two additional numbers on each of the five cards. The final solution must reveal the numbers 1 through 20, and each card must total the same number.

Solution on page 357.

(Need a clue? Turn to page 175.)

Clue to puzzle 10: Seven is the lowest possible score.

13.

SQUARE DEAL

Take the numbers 2 through 9 and square them (2 x 2, 3 x 3, etc.). No⬛
place each of these squared numbers in the nine vacant squares so tha▮
each row of four squares totals 102. One squared number (1 x 1), whic▮
appears four times, has already been positioned.

Solution on page 35▮

14.

...RO HOUR

...vel through this maze connecting each of the six spots with one
...tinuous meandering line. No passageway or intersection may be used
...re than once. Your starting and finishing points are located in the
...d-end passages.

Solution on page 361.

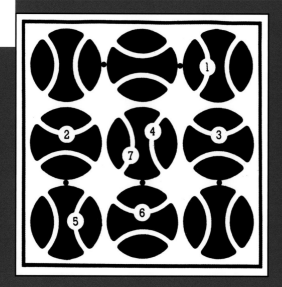

ROUND TRIPPER

For this nine-ball maze, connect the numbers 1 through 7 consecutively with one single continuous line and then return back to 1. Throughout your journey, you must pass through all eighteen ball seams exactly once. Further ground rules restrict normal passage between adjacent balls or walls next to balls to only once, and five dots positioned between balls block passage completely.

Solution on page 348.

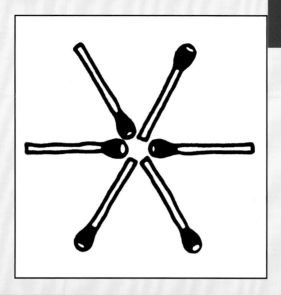

MATCH WITS 1

Here's a two-part matchstick puzzle designed to prove that half of eleven is six. First, rearrange two matches to reveal the number eleven. Then remove half of the matches to reveal the number six.

Solution on page 355.

Clue to puzzle 12: Each card must total forty-two.

17.

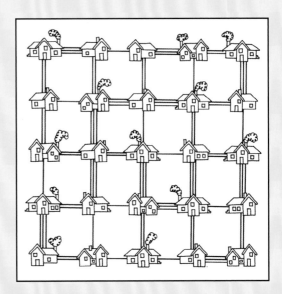

HOUSE CALL

Pick any house as your starting point and trace a route in the following
manner that visits all twenty-four of the remaining houses without ever
revisiting a single house: Follow one wire to the first house, follow two
wires to the second house, follow three wires to the third house, and
repeat this pattern over and over until all twenty-four houses are visited

Solution on page 35

(Need a clue? Turn to page 17

18.

?

28

496

8,128

130,816

2,096,128

THE
PERFECT
PYRAMID

What is the missing number that belongs on top of this pyramid and begins this progressively growing logical number sequence?

Solution on page 350.

19.

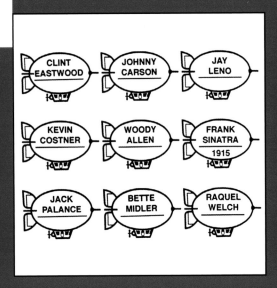

NINE GOOD YEARS

Hovering in nine blimps are nine talented superstars. They were born in the years 1915, 1920, 1925, 1930, 1935, 1940, 1945, 1950, and 1955. Correctly date each celebrity with the appropriate year of birth (as illustrated by Sinatra's airship) and you'll create a magic square in which each horizontal, vertical, and diagonal row of three blimps totals the same number. A couple of educated guesses should get you airborne.

Solution on page 357.

(Need a clue? Turn to page 181.)

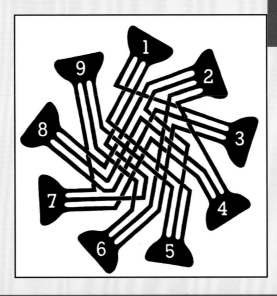

BOB N WEAVE

This numerical maze consists of nine numbered stations connected by fourteen crisscrossing pathways that intersect only at stations. Your task is to find a route that starts and finishes at station 1 and visits each of the remaining stations exactly once. At no time may any pathway be utilized more than once.

This puzzle has two possible solutions. Can you find both?

Solution on page 359.

Clue to puzzle 17: Finish at the center house.

21.

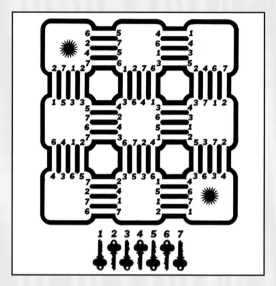

KEY DECISION 1

The numbered keys above correspond to the locked corridors in the puz
It is your challenge to select only three keys that will unlock the correct
corridors and allow passage from one sunburst room to the other.

Solution on page 3

22.

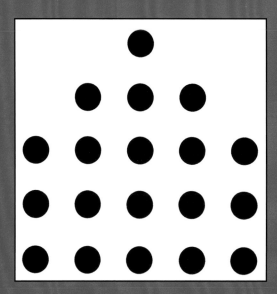

USE OF DOTS

37, 61, 91, _____

r challenge in this puzzle is to find the next number in the
thematical sequence above. Carefully study the illustrated house
dots, for it provides the key to the secret of the sequence.

Solution on page 348.

Clues to puzzle 19: Each row totals 5805.
Kevin Costner is the youngest.

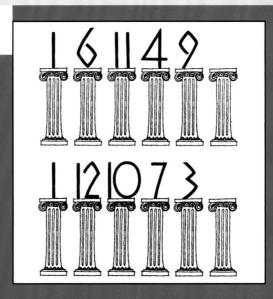

IT'S GREEK TO ME

These two puzzles would have perplexed even the cleverest of ancient
Greeks. Time will tell if you're clever enough to position a number atop
each of the vacant columns to complete these two separate numerical-
sequence problems.

Solution on page 351.

(Need a clue? Turn to page 184.)

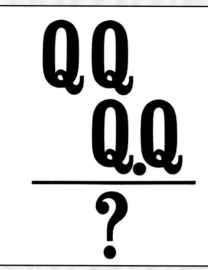

24.

MATCHING
4SUM

Illustrated above are two math problems in one. For one, you must add the numbers together. In the other, you must multiply them. Both problems must produce the identical sum and product. It is your task to determine the numerical value of Q and reveal the identical answers.

Solution on page 353.

25.

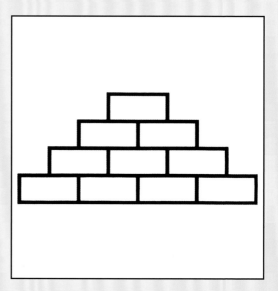

**THE
$10,000
PYRAMID**

Using only the number 4, place ten money amounts in the ten blocks of
this pyramid to total $10,000.

Solution on page 35

Clue to puzzle 23: Big Ben could help you solve these puzzl▶

26.

SITTING DUCKS

There are three different kinds of ducks in this puzzle. Position six more ducks on this two-dimensional pond so that each of the five horizontal and vertical rows will sport all three different kinds of sitting ducks.

Solution on page 357.

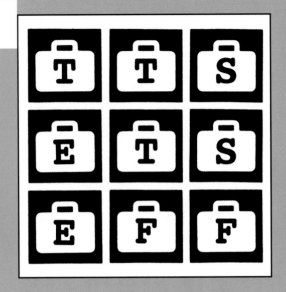

CASE CLOSED

Before you are nine cases labeled with the letters E, F, S or T. It is known that inside each case is a different number that begins with the letter seen on the outside of the case. Example: T could stand for 2, 3, 10, and so on. It is your challenge to determine all nine numbers to reveal a magic square in which each horizontal, vertical, and diagonal row of three cases totals exactly the same.

Solution on page 361.

(Need a clue? Turn to page 190.)

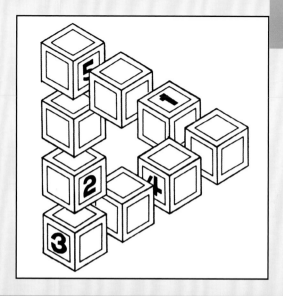

OPTICAL DIVERSION

Using the numbers 1 through 9 three times each, number the remaining surfaces of the cubes in such a way that each cube totals exactly fifteen. In doing so, you must also assure that each row of four cube surfaces in a straight row and facing the same direction (up, left, or right) must total twenty. Example: The two cube surfaces 3 and 4 above are in a straight line, facing left. There are nine such rows to be completed.

Solution on page 359.

29.

PHONY NUMBERS

Here is a coded word game in which the telephone is instrumental in converting numbers to letters. As seen on a touch-tone or dial phone, each of the numbers used in this puzzle can represent one of three different letters. It is your challenge to convert each line of numbers into a word that is related to its puzzle category. It takes one smooth operator to answer the call for each line of phony numbers in this collection of three categories.

Solution on page 349

CHILDHOOD GAMES

A•467726824
B•52257
C•6272537
D•53273764
E•824

THINGS YOU OBSERVE

A•7222284
B•5297
C•46543297
D•78277
E•2878667

ON AN AIRPLANE

A•2244243
B•66843
C•74568
D•73282358
E•327746637

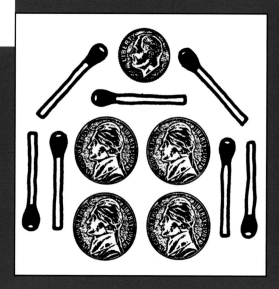

BURNING BRIDGES

Think of each match in this puzzle as a bridge that must be supported by two coins, one at each end. Your challenge is to arrange the four nickels, one dime, and seven matches to fulfill the following requirements: 1) Five matches must be supported by ten cents. 2) Two matches must be supported by fifteen cents. 3) No two matches may be supported by the same two coins.

Solution on page 353.

Clues to puzzle 27: Each row totals thirty-six.
The smallest number used is 4.

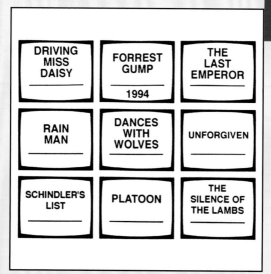

HOLLYWOOD SQUARES

Supply the correct year that each of these Academy Award-winning movies won their Oscars for Best Motion Picture and you'll create a magic square in which each horizontal, vertical, and diagonal row of three screens totals the same number. To get you started, it is given that Forrest Gump won in 1994.

Solution on page 351.

(Need a clue? Turn to page 195.)

32.

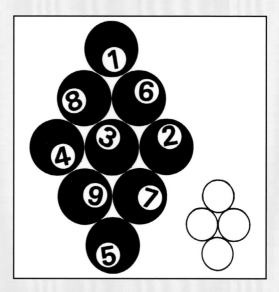

RERACKUM

This vertical diamond of nine billiard balls contains four smaller vertical diamonds of four balls (as seen in the sample above) that overlap and sha[...] various balls with other diamonds in the rack. It is your challenge to swit[...] the fewest number of balls to assure that each of the four diamonds tota[...] exactly the same number.

Solution on page 35[...]

33.

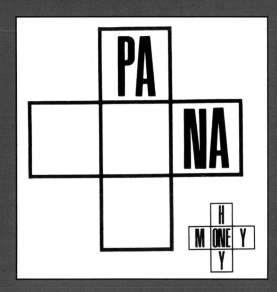

CROSS EXAMINATION 1

In the small sample puzzle illustrated, four letters (H, M, Y, Y) and one number (one) fill the five squares to create a mini-crossword number puzzle that spells MONEY across and HONEY down. Your task is to solve the partially completed puzzle above by positioning one number in the center square and a total of four letters in the remaining two squares to reveal two words that fit the following clues:

Across: A "touching" feature
Down: Government numbers

Solution on page 357.

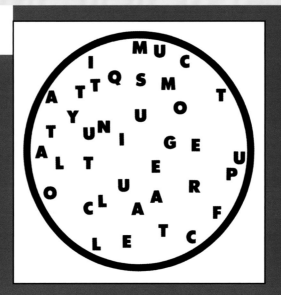

DIVIDE AND CONJURE

Use three straight lines to divide this circular playing field into six sections. If the lines are drawn correctly, the letters within each section can be unscrambled to reveal six related words, all associated with counting.

Solution on page 359.

(Need a clue? Turn to page 197.)

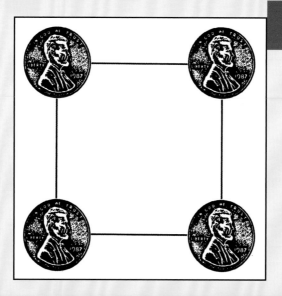

PENNY WISE

The centers of four pennies are positioned at the corners of the illustrated square. It is your task to reposition two pennies to create a new square exactly half the size of the existing square.

Solution on page 361.

Clues to puzzle 31: Each row of three screens totals 5970.
The oldest film won in 1987.

36.

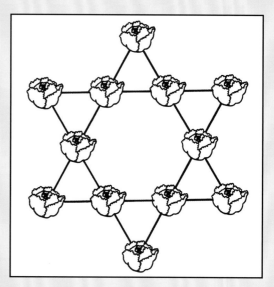

HEAD START

These twelve heads of lettuce are planted in such a way as to create six straight rows, each containing four heads of lettuce. Can you plant a garden using another configuration that fulfills these same requirements?

Solution on page 34

(Need a clue? Turn to page 20

37.

FLOATING HEDGES 2

Draw a continuous line through this maze that connects the numbers 1 through 8 consecutively. You may never travel the same passageway more than once.

Solution on page 351.

Clue to puzzle 34: Two of the unscrambled words are "quantity" and "figure."

38.

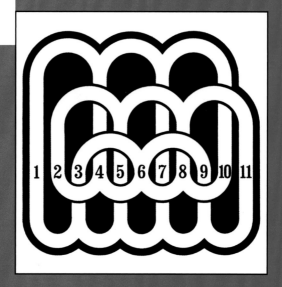

ARCHERY

Travel through this maze scoring the highest possible number of points. Begin by selecting a number of your choice. Your journey must begin and end at this number. Throughout your journey your path must always flow with the arches. Example: From "1" you may only travel to "3" or "4." At no time may you retravel any passage. Top score is sixty-six if you can visit all eleven numbers.

Solution on page 353.

(Need a clue? Turn to page 203.)

YANKEE INGENUITY

Six great Yankee ballplayers (Yogi Berra, Clete Boyer, Joe DiMaggio, Lou Gehrig, Mickey Mantle, and Babe Ruth) are each positioned on two base paths of this triple-decker infield. These players are most famous for wearing the numbers 3, 4, 5, 6, 7, and 8. Your challenge is to correctly match each uniform number with the correct Yankee to insure that each of the three different base paths will total exactly twenty-two.

Solution on page 355.

(Need a clue? Turn to page 205.)

40.

ROUND NUMBERS 1

Position one letter in each of the five between-spoke openings on this wag[
wheel. Do this in such a manner that three numbers are spelled out that
total thirteen. Words may be written clockwise and counterclockwise, and
in traditional crossword puzzles, individual letters may be shared. Example
On a larger wheel, four and five could be written: R-U-O-F-I-V-E.

Solution on page 35]

(Need a clue? Turn to page 20]

Clue to puzzle 36: Begin with a square four-by-four gr[
then eliminate four lettuce hea[

41.

MAGIC WORD SQUARES

...ch letter in this puzzle represents a different number from 0 to 9. It is your ...allenge to switch these letters back to numbers in such a way that each hor-...ntal, vertical, and diagonal row of three words totals the same number. Your ...tal for this puzzle is 1,515. It is known that TAB is the highest-scoring word ...d RAW is the second-highest-scoring word.

Solution on page 359.

(Need a clue? Turn to page 209.)

42.

ARROWHEADINGS

In this maze, your course headings are predetermined, and point values have been assigned to each passage. Starting from the bottom intersection, travel to each of the other five intersections and return to the beginning intersection with the lowest possible point score.

Solution on page 361.

(Need a clue? Turn to page 211.)

$$\frac{\text{WICKED}}{666}$$

WICKED NUMBER

At present this puzzle really totals only 601. That's because three of the letters in WICKED do not belong. You must eliminate the bogus letters and substitute the correct three letters to achieve the desired total.

Solution on page 349.

Clue to puzzle 38: Begin at number six.

44.

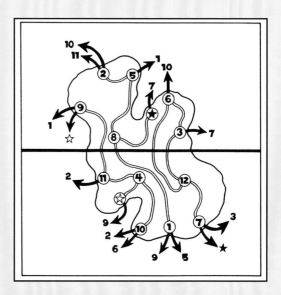

EQUATOR XING

There are twelve numerical destinations (1 through 12) on this tiny tropical island. You must start your journey at one of the two stars and then travel to each number on the map and ultimately finish at the other star. At no time may any number be visited more than once. Throughout your journey, you may only cross the equator a total of nine times: four by land, five by sea. Sea routes are illustrated by arrows that indicate your optional destinations.

Solution on page 35

45.

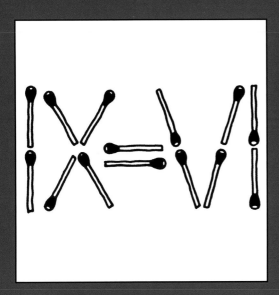

MATCH WITS 2

present we see an equation that incorrectly tells us that the Roman
numeral nine is equal to the Roman numeral six. Can you add three
additional matches to this equation to make both sides equal?

Solution on page 353.

Clue to puzzle 39: Ruth and Gehrig wore the lowest numbers.

6 SHOOTER

Travel through this maze connecting each of the six spots with one continuous meandering line. No passageway or intersection may be used more
than once. Your starting and finishing points are located in the dead-end
passages.

Solution on page 355.

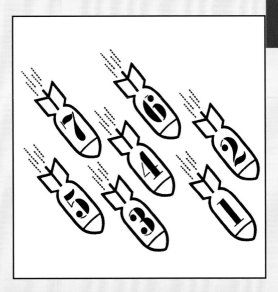

BOMBS AWEIGH

Five of the bombs in this puzzle are fully armed. Two of the bombs are unarmed and weigh half that of the armed bombs. From the following six groups of three bombs it is known that each threesome contains one unarmed bomb. Your task is to determine which two bombs are the lightweights.

1) 1, 2, 3   4) 4, 5, 6
2) 2, 3, 4   5) 5, 6, 7
3) 3, 4, 5   6) 6, 7, 1

Solution on page 357.

48.

THREE'S A CROWD

One way of making three threes total eleven is to combine two threes to make thirty-three and then divide by the final three to give the desired result of eleven. Can you find another way to make this threesome produce eleven?

Solution on page 36

Clue to puzzle 40: Begin by positioning O-N-E on the whe

49.

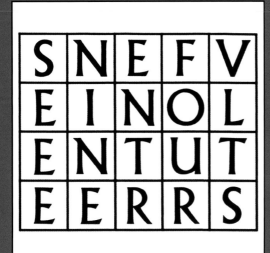

EVEN LETTERS

oss out seven letters to reveal two numbers.

Solution on page 349.

Clue to puzzle 41: DAD = 505.

50.

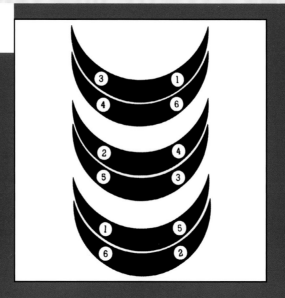

PAPER MOONS

Currently, six paper moons are arranged in such a manner that the two lefthand and two righthand circles from each pair total seven. It is your task to rearrange the six paper moons so that a new configuration is created in which six new pairs of two circles also total seven. Adjacent moons in the current configurations may not be adjacent in the new solution.

Solution on page 351.

(Need a clue? Turn to page 213.)

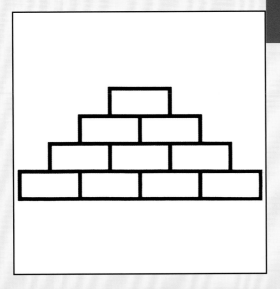

THE $1,000 PYRAMID

Using only the number 8, place ten money amounts in the ten blocks of this pyramid to total $1,000.

Solution on page 353.

(Need a clue? Turn to page 217.)

Clue to puzzle 42: Lowest score possible is forty-five points.

52.

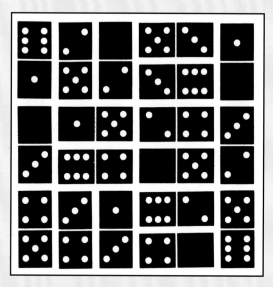

DOMINO SWITCHEROO

Switch the position of the fewest number of dominos in this puzzle to create a new six-by-six square in which no duplicate number of pips is repeated in any of the six columns or six rows. At present only the bottom row contains two identical four-pip squares.

Solution on page 35

(Need a clue? Turn to page 21)

53.

/EN STEVEN

ven and eleven are both odd numbers. Your task is to make both
mbers even without performing a single mathematical operation.

Solution on page 349.

**Clue to puzzle 50: Arrange all six paper moons into a doughnut
shape.**

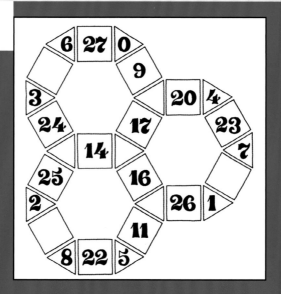

THREE RING CIRCUIT

When this puzzle is completely solved, it will reveal the numbers 0 through
27. All you have to do is position the remaining seven numbers to assure
that each of the three rings of twelve numbers totals exactly the same
number.

Solution on page 358.

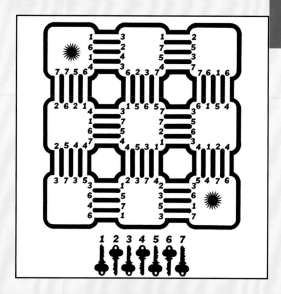

KEY DECISION 2

The numbered keys above correspond to the locked corridors in the puzzle. It is your challenge to select only three keys that will unlock the correct corridors and allow passage from one sunburst room to the other.

Solution on page 360.

56.

PATHFINDERS

Four pathfinders have coordinated their efforts in such a way that each individual can travel from start to finish using a different route. Each route must pass through exactly six intersections, revealing the numbers 1 through 6 (in any order). No path or intersection may be utilized more than once per route. Can you trace the routes of these four pathfinders?

Solution on page 3

57.

PAGEMASTER

Position page numbers on the remaining eight books in such a way that a magic square is formed in which each horizontal, vertical, and diagonal row of three books (six pages) totals exactly 111. Note: Books are always placed with the even-numbered page on the left.

Solution on page 350.

(Need a clue? Turn to page 221.)

Clue to puzzle 51: Think dollars and cents.

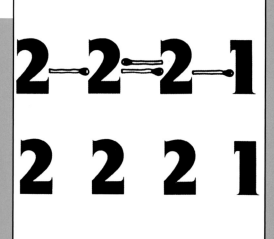

MATCH WITS 3

Two minus two does not equal two minus one. Rearrange only two matches to make the equation equal on both sides. Illustrate your answer with the bottom set of numbers.

Solution on page 352.

(Need a clue? Turn to page 224.)

Clue to puzzle 52: Only two dominos must be rearranged.

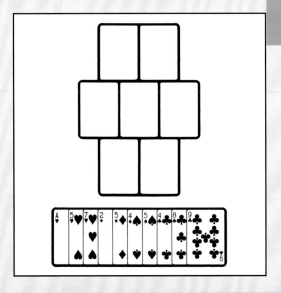

FIREHOUSE
SOLITARY

Position seven of the ten illustrated cards on the playing board as follows: 1) Identical suits may not appear in adjacent boxes. 2) Identical or consecutive face values may not appear in adjacent boxes. Ace is always low.

Solution on page 358.

60.

PYRAMAZE

Place the remaining numbers, from 1 to 12, in the vacant circles around
the pyramid so that: 1) The ends of all six crisscrossing passages total
the same number. 2) Each side of the pyramid adds up to a single number.

Solution on page 35

(Need a clue? Turn to page 22)

61.

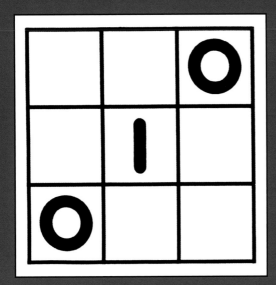

WIN-WIN SITUATION

You'll create a win-win situation if you're clever enough to fill the remaining squares with four numbers to complete this unique crossword-style number puzzle.

Solution on page 360.

(Need a clue? Turn to page 230.)

Clues to puzzle 57: The lowest page number is 2; the highest is 35.

62.

PHONY NUMBERS 2

Here is a coded word game in which the telephone is instrumental in
converting numbers to letters. As seen on a touch-tone or dial phone,
each of the numbers used in this puzzle can represent one of three
different letters. It is your challenge to convert each line of numbers into
a word which is related to its puzzle category. It takes one smooth
operator to answer the call for each line of phony numbers in this
collection of three categories.

Solution on page 350.

BREAKFAST FOODS

A•7287243
B•6286325
C•4727337848
D•72622537
E•2676352537

THINGS THAT ARE PULLED

A•82339
B•687253
C•8724567
D•83384
E•2277687

PANT-A-LOONY

A•25666377
B•267387697
C•386427337
D•56425377
E•752257

63.

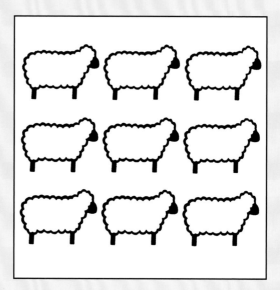

EWES YOUR HEAD

Nine shepherds herd nine flocks of consecutive numbers of sheep. Can y⬚
arrange these nine flock sizes in the nine ewes of this puzzle in such a w⬚
that each horizontal, vertical, and diagonal row of three ewes totals 199⬚

Solution on page 35⬚

(Need a clue? Turn to page 23⬚

**Clue to puzzle 58: For starters, mo⬚
the equals sign to the rig⬚**

64.

$$15X$$
$$+ 1Y$$
$$\overline{ 1Z}$$

DOUBLE TROUBLE

Here's a mathematical problem that has two correct and completely different solutions. You must solve for both solutions. In each case we're looking for fifteen of something (X) and one of something else (Y) that adds up to one of something else (Z). Example: If the problem were 3X + 2Y = 1Z, the answer could be 3 quarts + 2 pints = 1 gallon.

Solution on page 356.

(Need a clue? Turn to page 233.)

65.

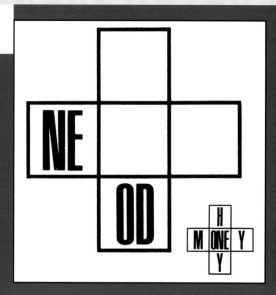

CROSS EXAMINATION 2

In the illustrated small sample puzzle, four letters (H, M, Y, Y) and one number (ONE) fill the five squares to create a mini-crossword number puzzle that spells MONEY across and HONEY down. Your task is to solve the partially completed puzzle above by positioning one number in the center square and a total of six letters in the remaining two squares to reveal two words that fit the following clues:

Across: As easy as ABC.

Down: It's all washed up.

Solution on page 354.

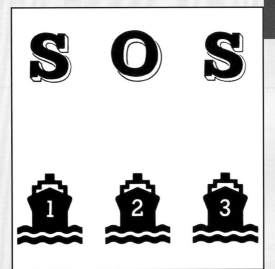

SAVE OUR SHIPS

Each of the ships in this puzzle has sent out a distress signal. Can you trace three paths from each ship that connect to each of the different letters of the S.O.S.? At no time may any of your lines cross one another or pass through ships.

Solution on page 360.

Clue to puzzle 60: The sums are thirteen and twenty-six.

67.

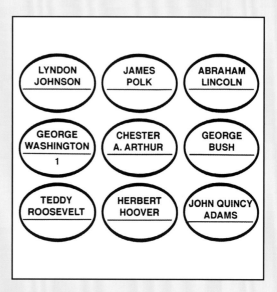

OVAL OFFICE FRENZY

Positioned in nine oval offices are nine presidents of the United States. These are the 1st, 6th, 11th, 16th, 21st, 26th, 31st, 36th, and 41st presidents. Correctly number each president's term of office (as illustrat by the Washington oval office) and you'll create a magic square in which each horizontal, vertical, and diagonal row of three offices totals the same number.

Solution on page 3!

68.

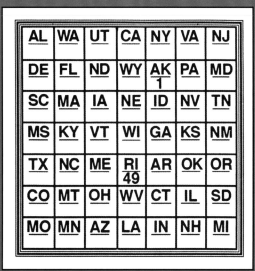

AL	WA	UT	CA	NY	VA	NJ
DE	FL	ND	WY	AK 1	PA	MD
SC	MA	IA	NE	ID	NV	TN
MS	KY	VT	WI	GA	KS	NM
TX	NC	ME	RI 49	AR	OK	OR
CO	MT	OH	WV	CT	IL	SD
MO	MN	AZ	LA	IN	NH	MI

∪ITED SQUARES OF AMERICA

⸮itioned above are the abbreviations of all forty-nine continental United ⸮tes. Alaska, the largest state in area, is number 1; Rhode Island, the ⸮allest, is 49. Rank the remaining continental states to create a magic ⸮are in which each horizontal, vertical, and diagonal row of seven ⸮ares totals 175. Even if you're not a geographic genius, a few educated ⸮sses will manifest your destiny.

Solution on page 354.

69.

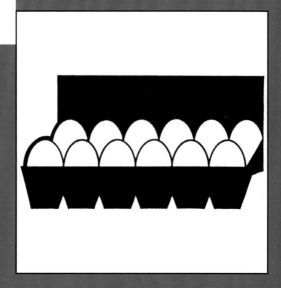

ONE EGGSTRA

As illustrated, at present this carton holds exactly one dozen eggs. How is it possible to position thirteen eggs in this same carton without breaking or scrambling a single egg? Placing two eggs in any single compartment is not allowed.

Solution on page 352.

Clue to puzzle 61: The numbers you position must be in the form of words.

FLUSTER 8

Travel through this maze connecting each of the seven spots with one continuous meandering line. No passageway or intersection may be used more than once. Your starting and finishing points are located in the dead-end passages.

Solution on page 360.

Clue to puzzle 63: The smallest flock is 661.

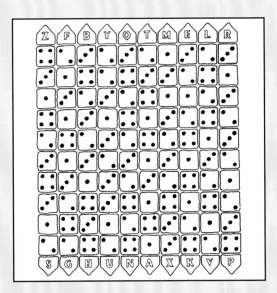

DICE DECIPHER

Using a four-number repetitive sequence (such as 2-4-1-3, 2-4-1-3, and so on), trace a path from any letter above to any letter below. You may move horizontally and vertically to any adjacent unused die.

Solution on page 3?

72.

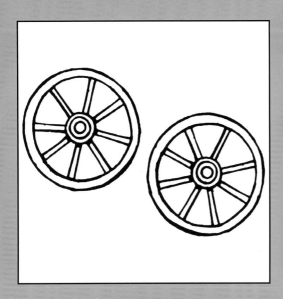

ROUND NUMBERS 2

Position one letter in each of the eight between-spoke openings of these wagon wheels. Do this in such a way that you spell out four numbers (two in each wheel) that, taken together, total thirty-one. The numbers in this puzzle must all be written in a clockwise manner, but just as in traditional crossword puzzles, individual letters may be shared. Example: Two and one would be written: TWONE.

Solution on page 354.

Clue to puzzle 64: In both solutions you must deal with "change."

73.

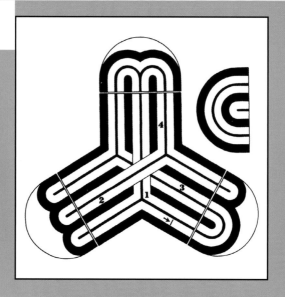

TRACE TRACK

The numbers in this puzzle show the current position of four cars on this crisscrossing racetrack. As the three outer turnabout panels are currently arranged, only car 1 can cross the finish line. Rearrange three of the four turnabout panels around the center section of track to construct a single unending track that utilizes all road surfaces and will allow all cars to finish in the order 1, 2, 3, 4. Cars may not pass one another on this final lap.

Solution on page 358.

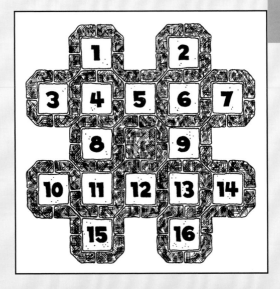

NUMERIC SHELVES

Rearrange the sixteen numbers in this puzzle to allow the two horizontal and two vertical rows of five squares to total the same number. There are twelve solvable totals. Your tasks are to construct the highest possible and lowest possible totals.

Solution on page 356.

75.

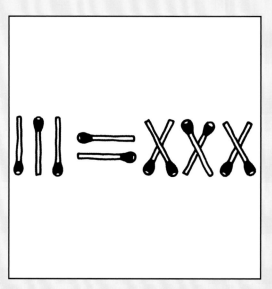

MATCH WITS 4

Move two matches to make this equation equal.

Solution on page 36(

76.

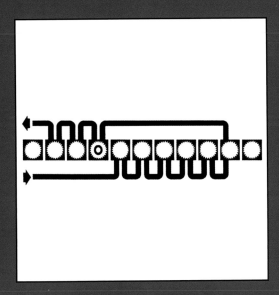

EN NUMBERS

ne of the eleven boxes above has already been filled. Fill the remaining
n boxes with ten numbers. If this is done correctly, the arrowed path will
ace the final solution, which is smaller than pi (3.141592...) yet one
rger than a number impossible to illustrate with Roman numerals.

Solution on page 356.

LUCKY LADY

Nine pairs of dice are positioned in nine horseshoes in this puzzle. The pips are missing from all but two dice. From the illustrated sixteen dice you must add the pips to the blank dice to satisfy the following conditions: 1) Each horseshoe must total a different number. 2) Each horizontal, vertical, and diagonal row of three horseshoes must total twenty-one. 3) Doubles may not appear in any horseshoe.

Solution on page 358.

4

PENCIL
PUZZLERS

1.

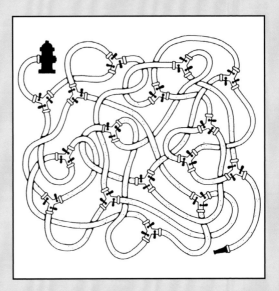

FIREMAN'S GATED "Y"

Each gated "Y" in this puzzle has three valves. Open the fewest number of valves to let the water flow from the hydrant to the nozzle. Play begins with all valves in the closed position.

Solution on page 36

(Need a clue? Turn to page 243

2.

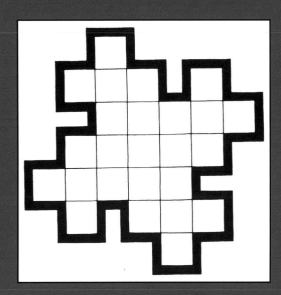

▲ACKOUT

blackening only five squares, divide this figure into five sections of equal
≥ and shape.

Solution on page 366.

(Need a clue? Turn to page 246.)

3.

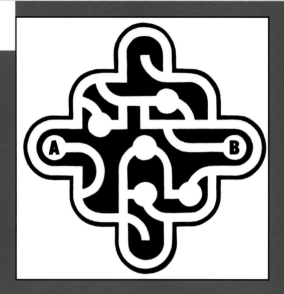

DUCK SOUP

Trace a path from A to B that travels through all five circular caverns. At no time may any passageway be used more than once.

Solution on page 368.

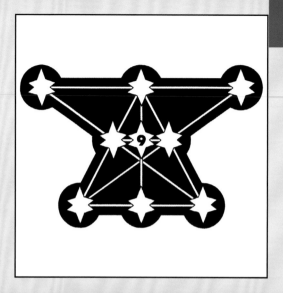

MAGIC STARS

Position the numbers 1 through 8 in the remaining vacant stars in such a way that each row of three stars totals fifteen.

Solution on page 370.

Clue to puzzle 1 : Twelve is the minimum number of valves.

5.

NUMBER NAVIGATION

There are thirty-seven stars in this galactic maze. Six of them have already been numbered and actually predetermine every step in your sta trek. Beginning at star 1, consecutively number every star in your journey so that you end at star 37. You may only travel from one adjacent star tip to the next, and at no time may you revisit any star.

Solution on page 37

6.

☐CTANGLE TANGLE

☐ing the information below, mark
☐h rectangle with a letter from
☐o J.

A	overlaps	D, E
B	overlaps	E, F
C	overlaps	D, G, I
D	overlaps	A, C, F

E	overlaps	A, B, H
F	overlaps	B, D, G
G	overlaps	C, F, J
H	overlaps	E, I
I	overlaps	C, H, J
J	overlaps	G, I

Solution on page 375.

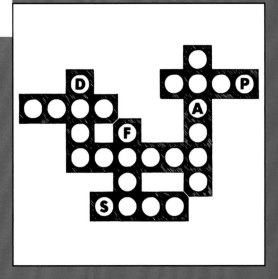

WORD WRESTLE

Solve this unique crossword puzzle by using each of the 26 letters of the alphabet only once. Five letters have been positioned for you. To fill in the rest of the puzzle, form the proper word associations from the seven clue words below and insert them on the puzzle grid. For example, the clue word YELLOW might bring to mind LEMON, COWARD, or MUSTARD.

The clues for this puzzle are: CHECKERS, CHESS, LINGERIE, SHIP, HORN, CRYSTAL, FINGERS.

Solution on page 373.

Clue to puzzle 2: The five blackened squares form the same shape as the five sections.

S
CAPE

Travel through this maze connecting each of the six dots with one continuous meandering line. No passageway or intersection may be used more than once. Your starting and finishing points are located in the dead-end passageways.

Solution on page 364.

9.

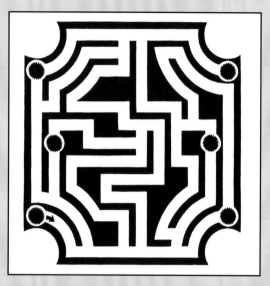

AZTREK

Trace a path through this maze that connects all six sunbursts with a single line. Begin your journey from the sunburst with the arrow at the lower left, and end at the upper right. At no time may any passageway be retraveled.

Solution on page 36

10.

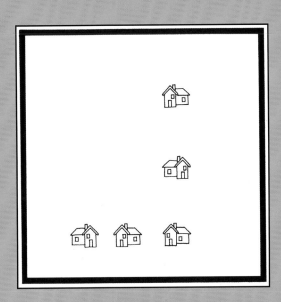

farmer left a will dividing his 400 acres of land among his five sons.
stipulates:

My oldest son receives 200 acres.

My second son receives 100 acres.

My third son receives 50 acres.

My youngest sons, twins, shall have 25 acres each.

rther, each parcel must be of the same shape and contain a house.

w must the estate be divided?

Solution on page 368.

LONG SHOT

Begin at the arrow and trace your way through this freewaylike maze of over- and underpasses with the goal of arriving at the winning "W," not losing "L," circle. Always keep with the graceful flow of the on-and off-ramps, just as you would on a real freeway.

Solution on page 372.

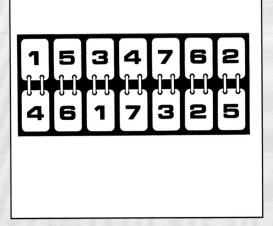

SCORE CARDS

These two rows of flip cards each contain the numbers 1 through 7 and total twenty-eight. Your task is to flip three cards from the top row over onto the bottom row (the back side of each card is blank), so that both rows will total one-half their present amount.

Solution on page 370.

13.

ARROWHEADINGS

In this maze, your course headings are predetermined, and point values have been assigned to each passage. Starting from the bottom intersection, travel to each of the other five intersections and return to the beginning intersection with the lowest possible point score.

Solution on page 37

(Need a clue? Turn to page 255

14.

‌EFTOVERS

‌s puzzle has two completely different and fascinating solutions. For
‌ch solution, blacken three different squares, then divide the remaining
‌rty-two squares into four sections identical in size and shape.

Solution on page 376.

15.

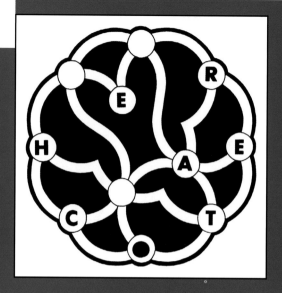

TONGUE TWISTER

This puzzle consists of two separate challenges: 1) See how many different words you can find that contain all the letters in the puzzle. 2) See how many of these words you can trace with one continuous line, starting at the black spot. No passage or intersection may be used more than once per word.

Solution on page 366.

16.

MANIFEST DESTINY

Examination of this forty-eight-star, American-flag pattern reveals twenty-four stars on its perimeter and twenty-four stars in its interior. How many stars would have to be added before this column and row phenomenon could occur again?

Solution on page 364.

Clue to puzzle 13: Lowest score is forty-six points.

17.

TWINKLE
SPRINKLE

Sprinkled throughout this maze are nine stars. Starting at one of the de
end stars, trace a continuous line linking all the stars and finish at the
other dead-end star. Do not pass over any path more than once.

Solution on page 37

18.

YSTERY CODE MANUSCRIPT

~ny experts say this code is impossible to crack, but don't you believe it.
~ elementary if you should stumble upon the correct technique.

Solution on page 374.

(Need a clue? Turn to page 259.)

KEY DECISION

The numbered keys above correspond to the locked corridors in the puzzle. It is your challenge to select only three keys that will unlock the correct corridors and allow passage from one sunburst room to the other.

Solution on page 368.

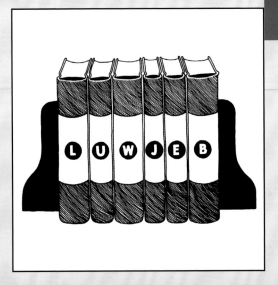

ENCYCLOPEDIA SHUFFLE

Take the books out of the rack and jumble them around. Now replace them between the bookends to spell a common six-letter word.

Solution on page 372.

(Need a clue? Turn to page 267.)

Clue to puzzle 18: The four J's in the puzzle represent the letters H, I, I, B—in that order.

21.

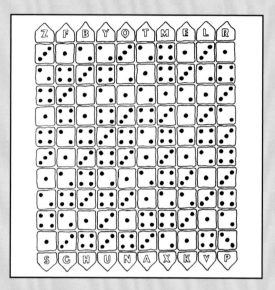

DICE DECIPHER

Using a four-number repetitive sequence (example: 2=4=1=3, 2=4=1=3 etc.), trace a path from any letter above to any letter below. You may move horizontally and vertically to any adjacent unused die.

Solution on page 37

22.

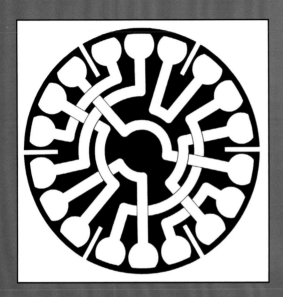

UEST TUBES

:cluding only the number 10, place numbers 1 through 19 in the eight-
:n bulbs of this puzzle. You must fulfill the following criteria: 1) Each pair
bulbs connected by a tube must total twenty. 2) The three bulbs in each
the six outer partitions must total thirty.

Solution on page 368.

23.

Y	A	P	A	O	E	L	P	P	A
A	E	C	P	D	A	C	O	V	E
I	N	H	O	L	E	M	E	A	N
R	L	E	N	E	P	R	T	A	I
E	E	R	R	Y	U	E	O	D	P
G	M	O	N	T	O	T	R	A	N
N	A	T	P	I	L	A	G	R	G
R	Y	A	E	U	A	W	C	A	E
R	H	C	M	R	T	N	A	P	E
E	B	L	U	F	D	A	E	R	B

TANGLE WORD

Using all 100 letters in this puzzle, reveal the related words and discover the mystery category. The words may be spelled out horizontally and vertically, forward or backward, many with twists and turns, but never scrambled. One word has been outlined to give you a start; partitioning off the rest is up to you. Letters may be used only once.

Solution on page 366.

THE BAFFLE R

Travel through this maze connecting each of the seven spots with one continuous meandering line. No passageway or intersection may be used more than once. Your starting and finishing points are located in the dead-end passageways.

Solution on page 370.

PYRAMAZE

Place the remaining numbers, from 1 to 12, in the vacant circles around
the pyramid so that: 1) The ends of all six crisscrossing passages total
the same number. 2) Each side of the pyramid adds up to a
single number.

Solution on page 364

(Need a clue? Turn to page 268

26.

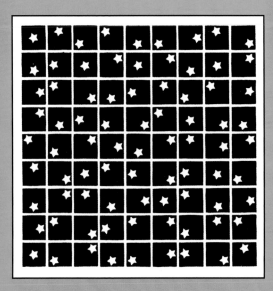

The stars in each square are located in one of nine positions: top left, top center, top right, left center, center, right center, bottom left, bottom center, and bottom right. Your task is to locate a three-by-three group of nine squares that contains one star in each position.

Solution on page 372.

27.

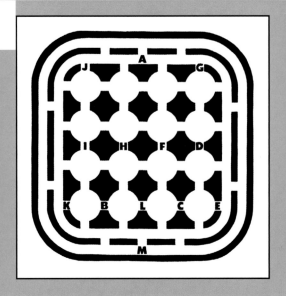

THE INNER COURSE

Draw a continuous line travelling alphabetically from A to M. All sixteen chambers in the inner course must be entered twice, but all pathways may be traveled only one time. Your line must never cross its own path.

Solution on page 374.

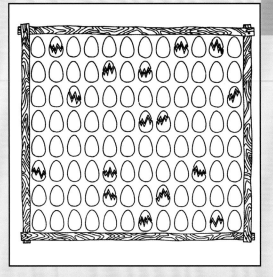

QUACK UP

Using only seven straight lines, divide this damaged crate of ninety-six duck eggs into eight compartments. Each compartment must contain a dozen eggs, including two broken ones.

Solution on page 376.

Clue to puzzle 20: Flip one of the books over.

29.

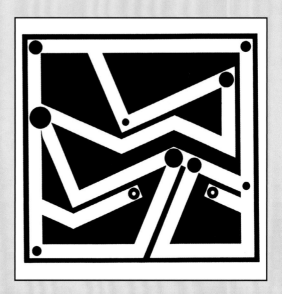

ABSTRACT
OF THE
ENCLOSURE

Travel through this maze connecting as many dots as possible with one continuous line. At no time may any passageway or intersection be retraveled. Start and finish at the "dotted" dots.

Solution on page 36

Clue to puzzle 25: The sums are thirteen and twenty-s

30.

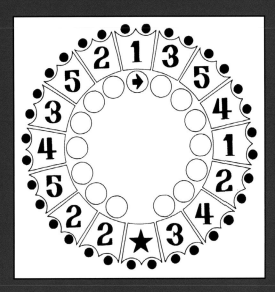

ᴛURNABOUT WHEEL

 gin at number "1" at the top of the wheel. Moving the indicated number
 spaces, you must land on each space on the wheel one time only and
 d your journey on the star space. Only the first directional arrow is
 en. You determine the direction of subsequent moves by placing an
 ow in the circle when you land on the adjacent space.

Solution on page 366.

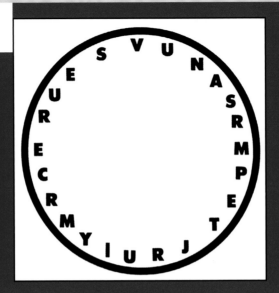

DIVIDE AND CONJURE

Use two straight lines to divide this circular playing field into four sections. If the lines are drawn correctly, the letters within each section can be unscrambled to reveal four related words.

Solution on page 368.

(Need a clue? Turn to page 274.)

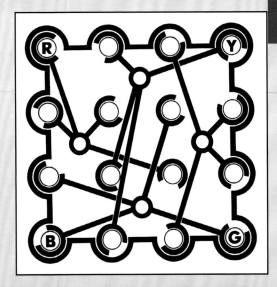

BUTTON
HOOKS

Four unusual devices grasp four buttons each in this puzzle. Your challenge
is to color the blank buttons so that: 1) Each device grasps a red, yellow,
blue, and green button. 2) Each horizontal, vertical, and diagonal row of
four buttons also contains a red, yellow, blue, and green button. The colors
of the four corner buttons are given.

Solution on page 370.

33.

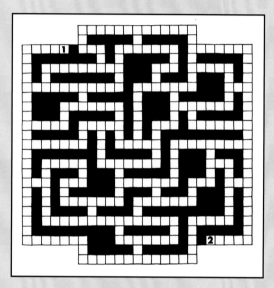

NOT A
CROSSWORD

Disguised as a crossword puzzle, this maze challenges you to draw a
continuous line from 1 to 2 passing through the greatest number of
squares. At no time may any square be revisited.

Solution on page 3

(Need a clue? Turn to page 27

34.

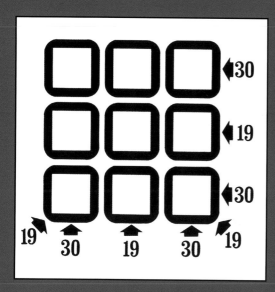

THE NINETEEN-THIRTY DEPRESSION

Here's a magic square puzzle that requires only two different numerical characters to solve. Position one of the two numbers in each of the nine squares so that the numbers 19 and 30 are revealed for each horizontal, vertical, and diagonal row of three squares as indicated. Negative numbers are not allowed.

Solution on page 376.

(Need a clue? Turn to page 279.)

35.

SPLIT-LEVEL

Look closely and you will see two interlocking puzzles above. Starting at each arrow on the left, trace separate paths through the maze to the finish arrows on the right. The total of one path must be twice that of the other. At no time may any passageway or number be revisited.

Solution on page 374.

Clue to puzzle 31: The words in this puzzle are really spaced out.

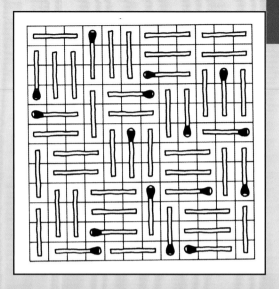

BLACK MATCHIC

Draw the match heads on the remaining thirty-two matchsticks in such a way that each horizontal and each vertical row of squares has the same number of match heads.

Solution on page 364.

(Need a clue? Turn to page 283.)

37.

ANT AGONIZER

Trace the only path this ant can take if he is to distribute the morsel of food equally into his seven storage dens. At no time may the ant travel through any passageway more than once during this task.

Solution on page 36

Clue to puzzle 33: It is possible to inclue all but twenty square

38.

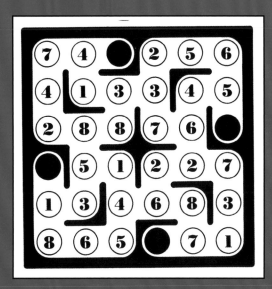

SPOT AND GO

Select two of the four black spots and trace a connecting path linking an equal number of spots of each numerical value. Example: If your course includes the numbers 2, 3, 5 and 8, it must contain the same amount of each of these numbers. Observe all partitions, traveling horizontally or vertically only to adjacent circles. At no time may any circle be used more than once.

Solution on page 368.

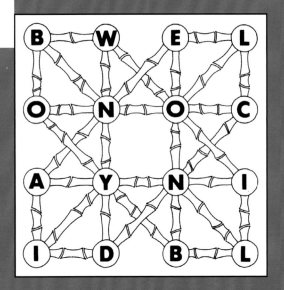

BAMBOOZLE

Many words can be formed by following this crisscrossing network of bamboo connectors. However, your challenge is to find only two words that can be considered opposite in meaning. Both words may start and end anywhere, but no letter or bamboo connector may be used more than once.

Solution on page 370.

Y ME?

Travel through this maze connecting each of the seven spots with one continuous meandering line. No passage or intersection may be used more than once. Your starting and finishing points are located in the dead-end passageways.

Solution on page 372.

Clue to puzzle 34: Think Roman numerals.

JUMBLE
SAFARI

Begin at the center of this maze and find your way to each of the sixteen
intersections. You may travel only in the direction indicated by the spears
and at no time may any intersection be revisited.

Solution on page 37

42.

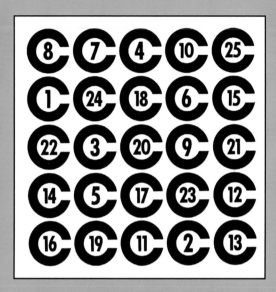

he numbers 1, 3, 7, and 18 form a perfect square and total twenty-nine
oints. Can you spot another perfect square, of any size, that will yield the
ghest possible score?

Solution on page 376.

43.

ALTERNATING OCCURRENCE

Beginning at the black spot on the far left, trace a path connecting each of the fourteen spots in the puzzle, alternating black and white, and ending with the white spot on the far right. None of the crisscrossing paths or intersections may be used more than once.

Solution on page 365.

ONE-TRACK MIND

Can you determine the three missing numbers to complete this numeric sequence?

Solution on page 367.

(Need a clue? Turn to page 286.)

Clue to puzzle 36: There must be four match heads per row.

45.

POT LUCK

Solving this maze requires tracing three different paths, one from A to A, one from B to B, and one from C to C. Together, the three paths must visit all six spots, but each path must connect a different number of spots. At no time may any passageway be traveled more than once.

Solution on page 36

(Need a clue? Turn to page 28*)

46.

TTING DUCKS

ere are three different kinds of ducks in this puzzle. Position six more
cks on this two-dimensional pond so that each of the five horizontal and
rtical rows will sport all three different kinds of sitting ducks.

Solution on page 371.

47.

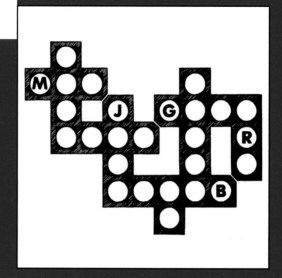

WORD WRESTLE 2

Solve this unique crossword puzzle by using each of the 26 letters of the alphabet only once. Five letters have been positioned for you. Fill in the rest of the puzzle by forming the proper word associations from the nine clue words below and inserting them into the puzzle grid. For example, the clue word YELLOW might bring to mind CANARY, AFRAID, PAD.

The clues for this puzzle are: GREEN, EGG, GUM, PIGEON, SHARKS, RUSSIAN, BLEND, METAL, SKY.

Solution on page 373.

Clue to puzzle 44: It truly requires a one-track mind.

RINGY DINGY

Each ring in this puzzle must link with only two other rings. Half of the over- and under-crossings are marked. Your task is to draw in the other thirteen.

Solution on page 374.

49.

DOWN AND OUT

Entering at the top, draw one continuous line connecting as many of the starbursts as possible before exiting at the bottom. At no time may any passage or intersection be retraveled.

Solution on page 36?

(Need a clue? Turn to page 290

Clue to puzzle 45: A links two spots
B links three, and C links one

50.

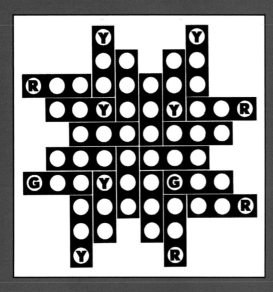

CROSSED SIGNALS

Each of the twenty traffic signals in this puzzle must include a red, yellow, and green bulb. The colors of twelve bulbs have been predetermined. Mark the colors of the other bulbs so that no two adjacent horizontal or vertical lights are the same color.

Solution on page 369.

51.

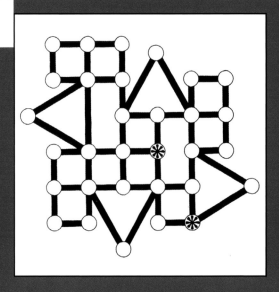

DEEP THOUGHT

Your challenge is to travel from one asterisk to the other in an even number of moves. There are numerous routes, but in each case a single passageway must always be used. Can you determine which of the forty-six avenues is the key link?

Solution on page 371.

Clue to puzzle 49: It's possible to link all but one starburst.

RINKY LINKS

Select six of the same lettered circles around the perimeter and draw three straight lines linking pairs of the circles to divide the rink into seven sections. Each section must contain only one black spot.

Solution on page 376.

53.

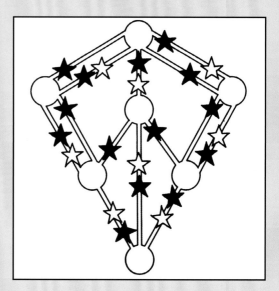

KITE STRINGER

Start and finish at the two white stars of your choice and connect all the stars in the puzzle with one continuous line. Passageways may be traveled only once. Intersections may be entered more than once, but you must not cross over your own path.

Solution on page 375

(Need a clue? Turn to page 296

54.

ur task is to subdivide this figure into six square pens that will allow
ch arrow to tally the same number of 6s. If an arrow passes through a
uare, all 6s within that square are counted.

Solution on page 367.

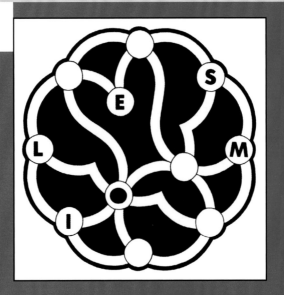

TONGUE TWISTER 2

This puzzle consists of two separate challenges 1) See how many different words you can find that contain all the letters in the puzzle. 2) See how many of these words you can trace with one continuous line, starting at the black spot. No passage or intersection may be used more than once per word.

Solution on page 369.

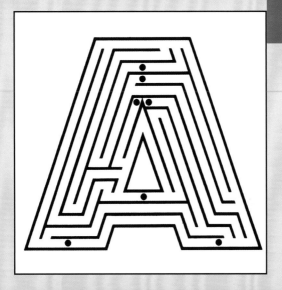

A
MAZING

Travel through this maze connecting each of the seven spots with one continuous meandering line. No passageway or intersection may be used more than once. Your starting and finishing points are located in the dead-end passages.

Solution on page 371.

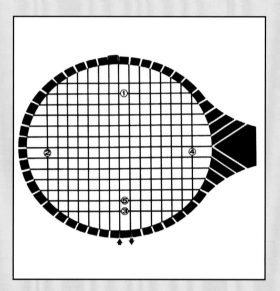

HIGH STRUNG

This tennis racket is strung with one continuous string. Trace its path, starting and finishing at the arrows. The five numbers must be strung in order, and you must exit and enter through adjacent eyelets. The same eyelet may be used more than once. Your first move is given.

Solution on page 36

Clue to puzzle 53: Which intersection
have an odd number of passageway

58.

FLATION

ne numbers 1 through 20 appear on the five balloons above, four
umbers on each balloon. Only two of the numbers, however, are visible
om this angle. Determine the hidden numbers on each balloon so that
e numbers on each balloon add up to the same total.

Solution on page 375.

(Need a clue? Turn to page 298.)

HIT THE SPOTS

Trace a path from A to Z that passes through each of the four spots.
At no time may any passageway be used more than once.

Solution on page 373.

Clue to puzzle 58: The numbers on each balloon total forty-two.

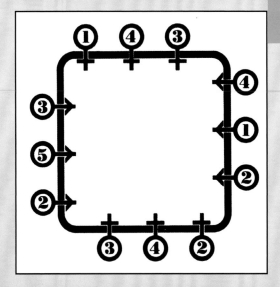

MAKING PASSES

At the sides of this park, six males stand ready to walk into it horizontally. Six females, starting from the top and bottom of the park, will be traveling vertically. The number within each male and female symbol determines how many persons of the opposite sex this person must pass in the park. Make these passes by lengthening the stem part of each symbol.

Solution on page 365.

61.

GOING TO PIECES

This is actually a devious maze disguised as a jigsaw puzzle. Starting at point A and ending at point B, it is your task to follow the black lines forming the pieces and encircle each of the six spots throughout the puzzle. At no time may the same line be traveled more than once.

Solution on page 36

62.

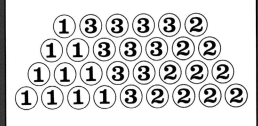

ch triangular rack of ten balls has a different numeric value. As the
cks appear above, the four horizontal rows total fifteen each. Can you
arrange whole racks to form five rows totaling twelve each?

Solution on page 373.

63.

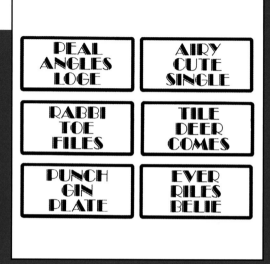

PEAL ANGLES LOGE	AIRY CUTE SINGLE
RABBI TOE FILES	TILE DEER COMES
PUNCH GIN PLATE	EVER RILES BELIE

WORD
WORLD

Each box is a different puzzle. For each puzzle, select a single letter from the alphabet and position it in each word in the box to create three new words. The title demonstrates how to play. Add an "L" to "WORD" to create the new word, "WORLD."

Solution on page 371.

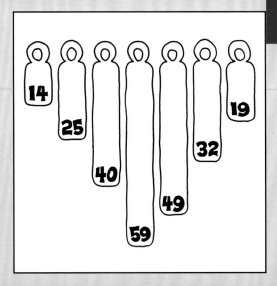

THE
WEIGHTING
GAME

Eliminate one of the weights in this puzzle. Now, form two different sets of three weights that total exactly the same amount.

Solution on page 369.

(Need a clue? Turn to page 306.)

65.

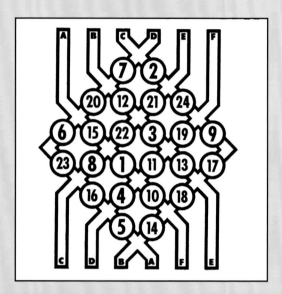

FIFTY GOING DOWN

Without ever moving in an upward direction, score a total of fifty points by traveling down each of the six lettered trails to the identical lettered finish below. Intersections may be used twice and lines may cross, but each number and trail may be used only once.

Solution on page 37

66.

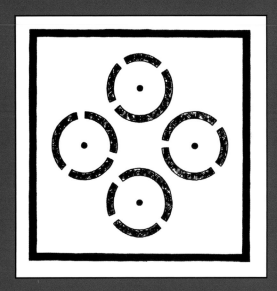

THE
ENTERING
DILEMMA

Using only five straight lines, travel through the most favorable openings
in the rings and link together all four center spots. All lines must remain
within the square boundary.

Solution on page 365.

67.

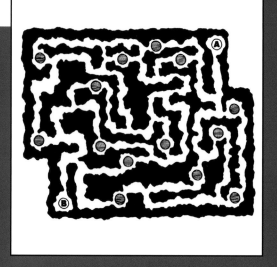

SWAMP MEET

Trace the route two explorers must travel if they are both to meet somewhere in the swamp after each has visited seven circular islands. One explorer leaves from site A and one from site B. At no time may any canal or island be traversed more than once.

Solution on page 367.

Clue to puzzle 64: Eliminate the 32 weight.

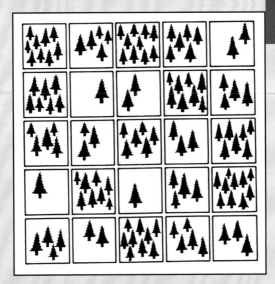

TIMBER TANTRUM

You plan to sell the timber rights to twenty-four of your twenty-five square acres of land to four lumber companies. How can the land be divided into four sections of six adjacent acres each so that each lumber company will receive an equal number of trees? One acre will be left over.

Solution on page 369.

(Need a clue? Turn to page 309.)

69.

UP & ATOM

Starting at position 1, find your way through each and every passageway of this cellular structure to connect each number in order, then return to your starting point. Although you will enter each intersection three times, at no time should your paths cross.

Solution on page 37

70.

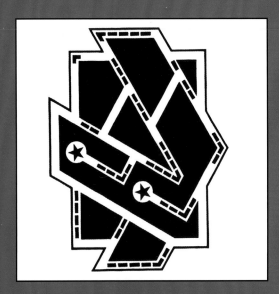

~~M~~AD DASH

~~Tr~~ace a path from one star to the other star so that it passes through
~~ex~~actly twenty-five dashes. You may not use any corridor more than once.

Solution on page 367.

**Clue to puzzle 68: The acre saved is a
corner lot.**

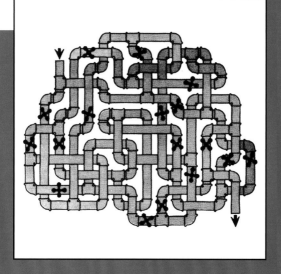

WATER
GATES

Open the fewest number of valves that will allow water to flow from one arrow to the other. Play begins with all valves in the closed position.

Solution on page 373.

N
DECISION

Travel through this maze and connect each of the six spots with one continuous meandering line. No passageway or intersection may be used more than once. Your starting and finishing points are located in the dead-end corridors.

Solution on page 365.

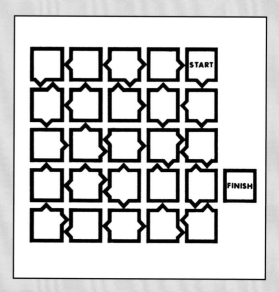

SQUARE ROUTES

In this puzzle, the box upon which you stop determines the direction of your next move. From any given position, you may advance any number of squares in a straight horizontal or vertical line in the direction of an arrow. For example, on your opening move you may travel only in a downward direction to one of the four squares below. The object is to make your way out of the maze to the finish square.

Solution on page 369

74.

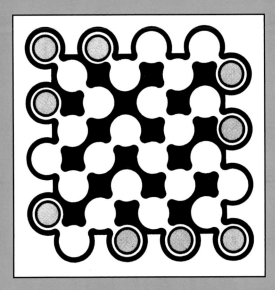

UMPING TO CONCLUSIONS

he distance between any pair of checkers can be measured by counting the
umber of circular jumps along the mazelike passages. Number the
heckers above from 1 through 9 so that the correct order of these twelve
hecker pairs, from least to most number of jumps apart, is as follows:

            1 and 7   5 and 9   1 and 3
            3 and 6   2 and 8   7 and 9
            2 and 9   5 and 7   2 and 6
            4 and 8   2 and 4   6 and 9

Solution on page 375.

75.

DETOUR AHEAD

Place a marker on the bottom star and maneuver it to the star above. Begin your journey by moving one, two, three, four, or five squares in an upward direction. The square on which you stop determines your next move: the arrow points out the direction, and the dots tell you how many squares to move. If a square contains two arrows, either route of travel may be selected.

Solution on page 365.

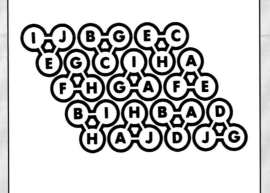

TRI ADD
DILEMMA

Each circle in this puzzle contains a letter. Each of these ten letters stands for a different number from 1 to 10. Substitute the correct number for each letter so that: 1) Each set of three circles totals fifteen. 2) Each horizontal row of six circles totals thirty. 3) Each of the six parallel diagonal rows of five circles totals twenty-five.

Solution on page 375.

77.

ASPHALT JUGGLE

Study the incomplete design of winding and crisscrossing roadways above. There are thirty manholes strategically positioned in the completed portions of the roadways. You must complete the road design by inserting four crisscross tiles and four curved roadway tiles to complete six roadways that start at the top cul-de-sacs and end at the bottom ones. Each completed roadway must contain exactly five manholes.

Solution on page 371

78.

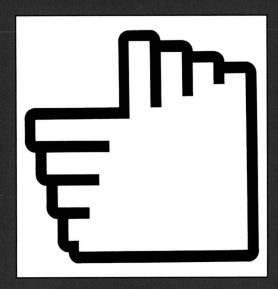

SQUARE IT AWAY

Divide the enclosed white area of this figure into the least number of pieces (eight) that can be rearranged to form a perfect square. Warning: This is a toughie! You may find it just as entertaining to skip all the frustration and spend the time examining the fascinating and unexpected solution.

Solution on page 373.

CHAPTER

1

Solutions

1) Knotholes 49, 34, and 17.

8)

15)

```
        1
  2     3
  4     5     6
  9     7     8
 11    10    12
 13    14    15
 ⌣     ⌣     ⌣
 39    40    41
```

27)

33)

40)

46)

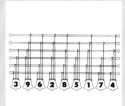

2)

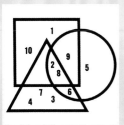

58)

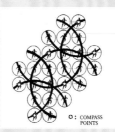

◊: COMPASS POINTS

9)

62)

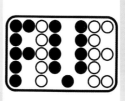

52)

69) The cakewalks are fifteen and sixty-three squares, respectively. There are an infinite number of larger cakewalks. Each increasing cakewalk is double in size plus one square.

16)

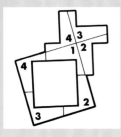

34)

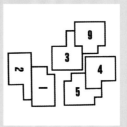

21) Each square totals twenty.

41) The number 72,930 is five times 14,586, and 14,586 is twice 7,293.

28) Variations of each solution exist.

47)

3)

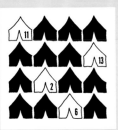

54)

10)

59) Each number represents a different color. Mirror images also correct.

22) Below is one of several maximum routes. The shortest route is 1, 10, 11, 12, 13, 9, 27, 28, 31, 32.

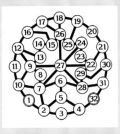

70)

29)

35)

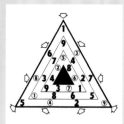

42)

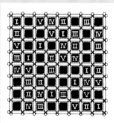

48) By opening the doors bearing the numbers 10, 6, 12, and 14, each row and column will total 20.

53) The numbers are 13 and 14:

$$13 \times 13 = 169$$
$$14 \times 14 = 196$$
$$169 + 196 = 365$$

60)

63) Since $^7/_8$ of an inch also represents the height of an equilateral triangle, 1 inch is the approximate base of this triangle. Hence, the total length of the strip is approximately 18 inches.

4)

DOWN 3   UP4   DOWN 1

11)

473	734	239
248	482	716
725	230	491

17)

23) The total of all four comparisons is forty gallons. Since each color appears twice in the four comparisons, half this total is the total of all five colors. In the first two comparisons, red, green, blue, and yellow total eighteen gallons. Therefore, orange must total two gallons. Using similar comparisons, we find that red totals three gallons, blue totals four gallons, green totals five gallons, and yellow totals six gallons.

32)

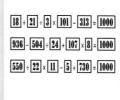

$$18 + 21 \div 3 \times 101 - 313 = 1000$$
$$936 - 504 \div 24 + 107 \times 8 = 1000$$
$$550 \div 22 \times 11 - 5 + 730 = 1000$$

36)

43)

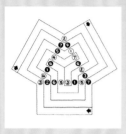

49) Mirror images also correct.

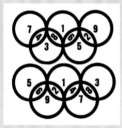

55)

64) The remaining seven commands must be given in the following order:

Six squares right flank march.

Ten squares to the rear march.

Seven squares left flank march.

Four squares right flank march.

Thirteen squares to the rear march.

Fourteen squares left flank march.

Five squares left flank march.

66)

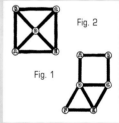

Fig. 2

Fig. 1

5)

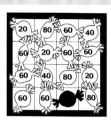

12)

18)

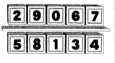

71) The direction in which a "V" slot points determines the sunspot or sunspots in which a number must be totaled. The example below illustrates that the number in the "V" slot marked with an arrow must be totaled in the two sunspots identified with asterisks.

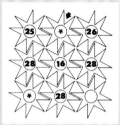

72)

24)

30)

Sample on puzzle page:

1, -, -, 2, -, 3, 4, -, -, -, 5, -, -, 6, -, 7, 8.

Further solutions:

1) 1, 2, -, 3, -, -, 4, -, -, -, 5, 6, -, 7, -, -, 8.
2) 1, -, 2, -, -, 3, -, 4, -, -, -, 5, -, 6, 7, -, 8.
3) 1, -, 2, 3, -, 4, -, -, -, 5, -, 6, -, -, 7, -, 8.
4) 1, -, -, 2, -, -, 3, -, -, 4, -, -, -, 5, 6, 7, 8.
5) 1, 2, 3, 4, -, -, -, 5, -, -, 6, -, -, 7, -, -, 8.

37) Shown, twenty-one intersections. A total of forty-two spots are required to create 210 intersections. That's one-quarter of the total spots times the maximum intersections per line (1/4 x 42 x 20 = 210).

44)

6)

13) Cut four threads.

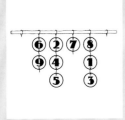

50) The top-right and bottom-left shapes were switched.

56)

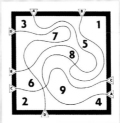

61) Numbers 3, 37, and 111.

67) As the gears appear from right to left:

233
▼
896
▼
594
▼
675
▼
483

19) The lightning bolt equals the star. Using the letters L, M, and S to represent lightning, moon, and star, the following equations provide the proof:

given:	LMM = LLLSSSS
reduce to:	MM = LLSSSS
given:	LLLM = LLSSSS
therefore:	MM = LLLM
reduce to:	M = LLLL
therefore:	LMM = LLLLLLL
therefore:	LLLSSSS = LLLLLLL
reduce to:	SSSS = LLLL
therefore:	S = L

25) Pie 1: $4^{38}/76\% + 95^{1}/2\% = 100\%$
Pie 2: $8^{27}/54\% + 91^{3}/6\% = 100\%$

38)

45)

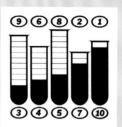

51) The correct sequence is: 3, 0, 4, 1, 5, 2, 6, 3, 7, 4, 8, 5, 9, 6, 10. Key: Subtract 3, add 4, subtract 3, add 4, etc.

73) Both craftsmen can solve in four pieces.

The glass cutter can solve with two pieces by flipping over either piece.

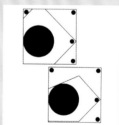

7) This puzzle is solved by turning over, or "cap-sizing," the 9/8 hat. Now, 8/6 + 10/6 = 3.

14)

20)

26) A stride of $52^{1}/_{2}$ inches is reached on the forty-second step.

68)

74)

6	triangles	+	3	=	9
12	triangles	-	3	=	9
3	triangles	x	3	=	9
27	triangles	÷	3	=	9

31)

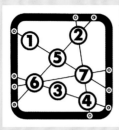

65)

$$\boxed{568} \div \boxed{71} + \boxed{4} \times \boxed{103} - \boxed{236} = \boxed{1000}$$

$$\boxed{24} + \boxed{618} \times \boxed{15} \div \boxed{9} - \boxed{70} = \boxed{1000}$$

$$\boxed{203} - \boxed{65} \times \boxed{64} + \boxed{168} \div \boxed{9} = \boxed{1000}$$

39)

57) The three numbers are one, two, and four,
The divisions of each respective row are:

      Row 1:   7, 7, 7

      Row 2: 12, 6, 3

      Row 3: 16, 4, 1

2

Solutions

1)

13) The best possible solution requires 7,979 steps by each marker. This is found by determining the lowest common denominator and subtracting 1:

$(19 \times 20 \times 21) - 1 = 7,979$

21)

28)

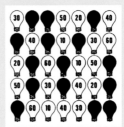

33)

40)

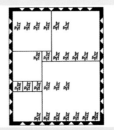

2) Variations of lap A exist.

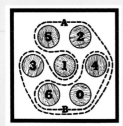

8)

48)

IT'S GREEN	FRUIT
1) money	1) grape
2) grass	2) apple
3) jade	3) banana
4) emerald	4) lemon
5) cactus	5) tangerine

PLANETS
1) Mars
2) Venus
3) Neptune
4) Uranus
5) Earth

58)

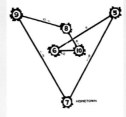

14) The missing homographs are:

ASSOCIATE

INTIMATE

INVALID

CONTEST

EVENING

RECORD

35) There are 49 steps.

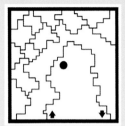

22)

63)

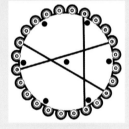

29)

69) Hank Aaron

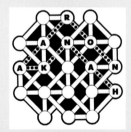

3)

Place	Dog
1st	4
2nd	3
3rd	6
4th	1
5th	2
6th	5
7th	7

41)

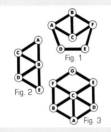

46)

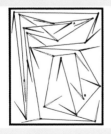

53) Each column and row has its own progressive sequence.

59) The topic is vegetables.

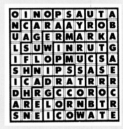

64)

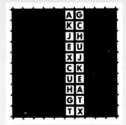

7)

10)

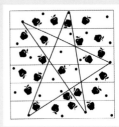

16) Diagonal flip-flop also correct.

5 A	6 B	4 C
7 D	3 E	8 F
2 G	9 H	1 I

23) MONEY TALK NATIONAL PARKS

    A) dough   A) Yosemite

    B) bread   B) Everglades

    C) greenback C) Shenandoah

    D) peanuts   D) Glacier

    E) wampum   E) Yellowstone

       DIG IT

       A) dugout

       B) trench

       C) canal

       D) well

       E) foxhole

37)

68) It is possible to spell the words SILENCE and LICENSE; however, only SILENCE can be traced.

4)

42)

18)

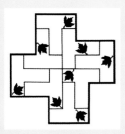

47)

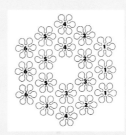

30)

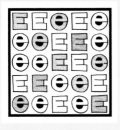

54)

11) Solution uses 103 circles.

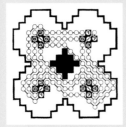

36) SUNDIAL, WRISTWATCH, SANDGLASS.

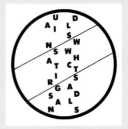

24) "Don't tread on me."

43) One of four mirror and flip-flop images.

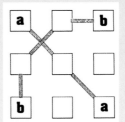

65)

| Left shade raised three rows. | Middle shade raised four rows. | Right shade raised two rows. |

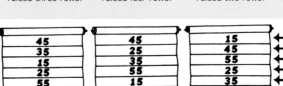

5) Mirror image also correct.

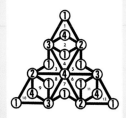

17) Rotational and mirror images also correct.

31)

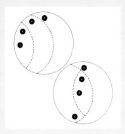

50)

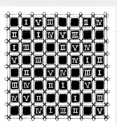

56) 1) Shown below 2) Trails 1 and 2 (6)
3) Trails 1, 2, and 4 (2)

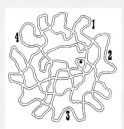

66)

9) The candy jars hold:

13 peppermints

39 jelly beans

52 red-hots

117 gum balls

26) The commander has 120 tanks to position in ten columns and twelve rows (or vice versa) for forty on the perimeter and eighty in reserve.

38) One of many solutions.

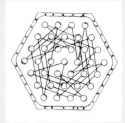

44) Total letter count below: 279. Higher scores exist using more obscure words.

A-A   abracadabra 11

B-B   bathtub 7

C-C   commercialistic 15

D-D   departmentalized 16

E-E   extinguishable 14

F-F   flameproof 10

G-G   gerrymandering 14

H-H   homestretch 11

I-I   isthmi 6 (isthmus, pl.)

J-J   ---

K-K   knickknack 10

L-L   lackadaisical 13

M-M   microorganism 13

N-N   nationalization 15

O-O   obbligato 9

P-P   proprietorship 14

Q-Q   ----

R-R   revolutionizer 14

S-S   supercalifragilisticexpialidocious 34 (from Mary Poppins)

T-T   transcendentalist 17

U-U   unau 4 (a two-toed sloth)

V-V   -----

W-W   wheelbarrow 11

X-X   Xerox 5

Y-Y   youthfully 10

Z-Z   Zardoz 6 (1974 Sean Connery film)

6)

49)

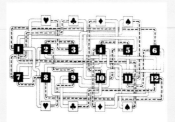

19) Your move, shaded, guarantees a win in three moves. Illustrated is one of two possible outcomes.

62) From A travel in sequence to destination squares 10, 13, 15, 5, and then to B.

67)

12)

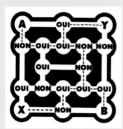

39)

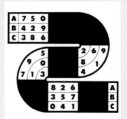

25)

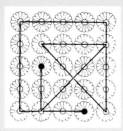

45)

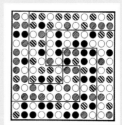

34) The letters are R, G, and C.

71)

20)

51) The words are DEVIL and LIVED, TIME and EMIT.

55)

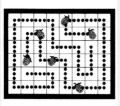

61)

1) Move 7 under to touch 8-9.

2) Move 8 over to touch 4-6.

3) Move 1 down to touch 6-8.

4) Move 8 down to touch 1-7.

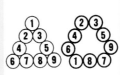

70) This puzzle can also be solved using forty-five disks. Try your luck.

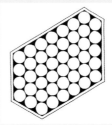

72) The cakewalks are sixteen and sixty-four squares, respectively. There are an infinite number of larger cakewalks. Each increasing cakewalk doubles in size.

15)

52)

27) A) VII, V, VI, IV, X, III, I, VIII, II, IX
B) IV, VIII, III, V, IX, VII, X, VI, I, II
C) VII, V, VI, IV, IX, III, X, VIII, I, II
D) IV, VIII, III, V, X, VII, I, VI, II, IX

57)

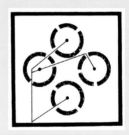

32) Other solutions may exist for each word.

60)

1) With the maze upside down, the task becomes elementary.

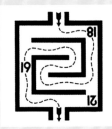

8)

6 x 6 = 9 boards
4 x 4 = 25 boards
2 x 2 = 49 boards
‾‾‾‾‾‾‾‾‾‾‾‾‾‾‾‾‾‾
         83 total

15)

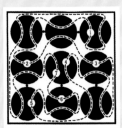

22) Each sequenced number represents the number of dots in progressively larger and proportional houses of dots whose width is always equal to its own height. The missing number is 127, a house of dots whose width and height measure thirteen dots.

29) CHILDHOOD GAMES

A)   hopscotch

B)   jacks

C)   marbles

D)   leapfrog

E)   tag

THINGS YOU OBSERVE

A)   sabbath

B)   laws

C)   holidays

D)   stars

E)   customs

ON AN AIRPLANE

A)   baggage

B)   movie

C)   pilot

D)   seatbelt

E)   earphones

36)

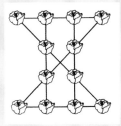

43) Eliminate W, K, and E. Substitute the Roman numerals V, X, and L.

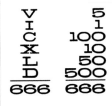

49)

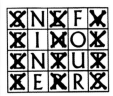

53) Remove S from seven, and E and L from eleven.

2)

9) Reflection also correct.

18) The missing number is 6. All of the numbers on this pyramid are "perfect." A perfect number is a number whose total divisions equal itself. Ex: 1, 2, 3 are all divisors of 6 and total 6. 1, 2, 4, 7, 14 are all divisors of 28 and total 28. There are only six perfect numbers between 1 and 3,000,000.

57) Reflection image also correct.

62) BREAKFAST FOODS

A)   sausage

B)   oatmeal

C)   grapefruit

D)   pancakes

E)   cornflakes

THINGS THAT ARE PULLED

A)   taffy

B)   muscle

C)   trailer

D)   teeth

E)   carrots

PANT-A-LOONY

A)   bloomers

B)   corduroys

C)   dungarees

D)   knickers

E)   slacks

23) Both puzzles are solved by using the face of a clock:

1) Starting at 1, travel in a clockwise direction, counting every fifth number.

2) Starting at 1, travel in a counterclockwise direction, moving first one number, then two numbers, then three, four, and five.

The use of the twelve-hour division and the modern clock face did not exist in ancient Greece. The mechanical twelve-hour clock was invented in the 1300s.

31)

37)

44) From the dark star, proceed to 7, 3, 12, 6, 10, 2, 5, 8, 1, 9, 11, 4, white star. Reverse order also correct.

50)

3)

63) Reflections and rotations also correct.

10)

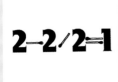

69)

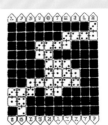

58) Two minus two halves equals one.

71)

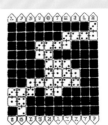

17)

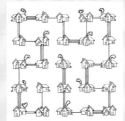

24)

11

1.1

―――

12.1

30)

38)

Begin at 6. End at 6. Score is sixty-six.

45) SIX equals VI.

51)

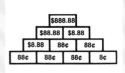

4)
    1)   533 years 4 months
    2)   333 years 4 months
    3)   133 years 4 months

11)

56)
    A)   2, 3, 6, 4, 5, 1
    B)   5, 6, 2, 1, 4, 3
    C)   5, 6, 2, 3, 4, 1
    D)   5, 6, 3, 4, 2, 1

65) NETWORK/DRIFTWOOD

68) Hawaii ranks 47th if you count all fifty states.

AL	WA	UT	CA	NY	VA	NJ
28	20	12	3	30	36	46
DE	FL	ND	WY	AK	PA	MD
48	26	17	9	1	32	42
SC	MA	IA	NE	ID	NV	TN
40	45	23	15	11	7	34
MS	KY	VT	WI	GA	KS	NM
31	37	43	25	21	13	5
TX	NC	ME	RI	AR	OK	OR
2	29	39	49	27	19	10
CO	MT	OH	WV	CT	IL	SD
8	4	35	41	47	24	16
MO	MN	AZ	LA	IN	NH	MI
18	14	6	33	38	44	22

72) Reflections and rotations also correct.

            THREE
            EIGHT
            NINE
       + ELEVEN
        THIRTY-ONE

16) From Roman numeral eleven, illustrated (XI), remove the three matches below the dotted line to reveal Roman numeral six (VI).

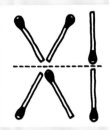

25)

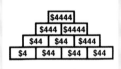

32) The rack is correct as is. Each diamond totals exactly twenty-one. Simply spin the 6 and 9 balls 180 degrees to reveal their correct orientations.

39) In home run order:

Top: 7, 3, 8, and 4

Middle: 5, 3, 8, and 6

Bottom: 5, 7, 4, and 6

3	Ruth
4	Gehrig
5	DiMaggio
6	Boyer
7	Mantle
8	Berra

46)

52) Switch the one/zero domino with the four/zero domino.

5)

60)

64)

15 pennies	15 nickels
+ 1 dime	+ 1 quarter
1 quarter	1 dollar

74) Many variations exist for both solutions. The lowest is 37.

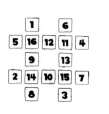

The highest is 48.

76) The concept of zero cannot be illustrated with Roman numerals. The path reveals "NUMBER ONE."

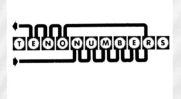

12)

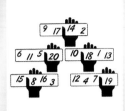

19)

26)

33) ANTENNA/PATENTS

40) Reflections and rotations also correct.

```
     ONE
     TWO
   +TEN
THIRTEEN
```

47) Numerically, the lightweights must be separated by two armed bombs. Since 1, 2, and 7 must be armed, the unarmed bombs must be 3 and 6.

6) It's easy once you realize that the two fathers and two sons total only three people: a grandfather, a son, and a grandson.

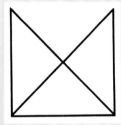

54) One of several possible solutions.

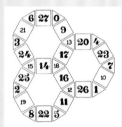

59) One of several variations.

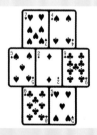

67)

73)

77)

13) Numbers 9 and 25 may be reversed.

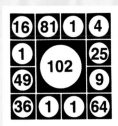

20) 1, 3, 6, 2, 8, 4, 7, 9, 5, 1
        or
1, 7, 4, 2, 8, 3, 6, 9, 5, 1

28)

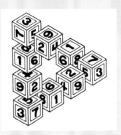

34) SUM, COMPUTE, FIGURE, CALCULATE, TOTAL, QUANTITY.

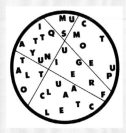

41)

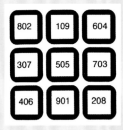

48) Combine the smallest and largest 3 to create the illustrated number eight. Now 8 + 3 = 11.

55) Keys needed: 1, 3, 5.

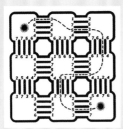

61)

66) Variations of this solution exist, but in each case one of the lines must pass through the letter "O," otherwise this puzzle is impossible to solve.

70)

75) This Roman numeral equation reads: 100 = 10 x 10.

7)

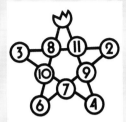

27)

14)

35) Rotations also correct.

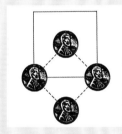

21) Keys needed: 2, 3, 4.

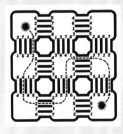

42)

4

Solutions

1)

25)

8)

29)

16) Twelve stars must be added to the American-flag, forty-eight-star field to total sixty stars. The correct arrangement is five rows of twelve stars.

36)

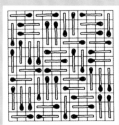

43) One of three possible solutions.

66)

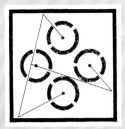

57)

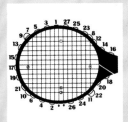

72)

60)

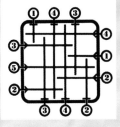

75)

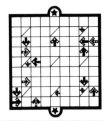

2)

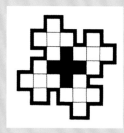

23)

9)

30)

15) It is possible to spell and trace both of these words: CHEATER, TEACHER.

37)

44) The missing numbers are 1, 1, and 11. The key: Add any two adjacent numbers; this total always appears two boxes to the right of the adjacent numbers.

49)

54)

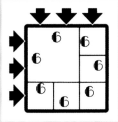

61)

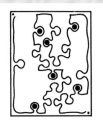

67)

70)

3)

10)

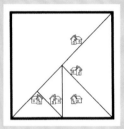

19) Keys needed: 2, 6, 7.

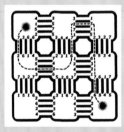

22)

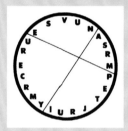

31) Unscrambled words: VENUS, MARS, JUPITER, MERCURY.

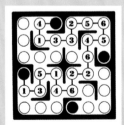

38)

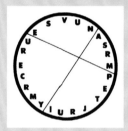

45)

50)

55) It is possible to spell these four words: SLIME, LIMES, SMILE, MILES; however, only the last two words can be traced.

64) With the 32 weight eliminated, each set below totals 103.

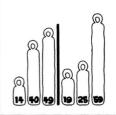

68)

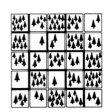

73)

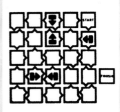

4) One of four solutions. "Mirror images also correct."

12)

17)

24)

32)

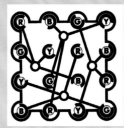

39) The words are COWBOY and INDIAN.

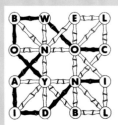

46)

51) The avenue marked by arrows must be traveled in order to solve this puzzle.

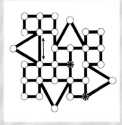

56)

63)

PEDAL	HAIRY
DANGLES	CHUTE
LODGE	SHINGLE
RABBIT	TITLE
TOTE	DETER
FILETS	COMETS
PAUNCH	FEVER
GAIN	RIFLES
PALATE	BELIEF

69)

77)

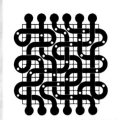

5)

26)

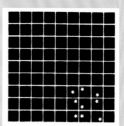

11)

33) Avoid the twenty squares marked with circles.

20) When flipped over, book "W" becomes "M." The solution is now obvious. The word is JUMBLE.

40)

7)

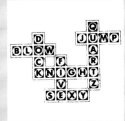

47)

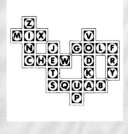

59)

62)

71) Turning on three valves will allow water to flow.

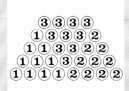

78)

13)

18) Each letter can be decoded by counting backward in the alphabet by the number of the position of that letter in a given word. For example, if P is the fifth letter in a word, counting backward five letters will reveal it to be the letter K. The message reads: "Many experts say this code is impossible to crack."

27)

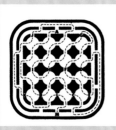

35) Any top path that connects all numbers is correct.

41)

48)

6)

65)

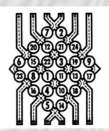

53) Many routes exist, but stars A and B will always begin and end each string.

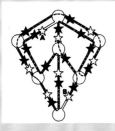

74)

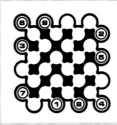

58) The numbers on each balloon must total forty-two. They must be grouped as follows:

1) 7, 12, 4, 19
2) 16, 8, 3, 15
3) 13, 1, 10, 18
4) 5, 20, 6, 11
5) 14, 9, 17, 2

76)

14)

34) ROMAN NUMERALS

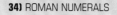

21) Sequence of die: 2, 4, 3, 1.

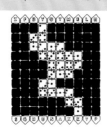

42)

28)

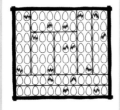

52)

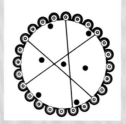

About the Author

If the world's greatest magician was Harry Houdini, and the world's greatest detective was Sherlock Holmes, then surely the world's greatest puzzle and game master is Steve Ryan, recognized as one of the most prolific creators of puzzles in the world, with more than 12,000 IQ boosters to his credit.

This virtuoso of vexation has been inventing games and puzzles since childhood. Early in his career he found a market for his creations at Copley News Service, where his *Puzzles & Posers* and *Zig-Zag* features have appeared for more than twenty-five years.

Ryan's creative genius also catapulted him into television, where he co-created and developed the TV game show **"Blockbusters"** for television's most prestigious game show packager, Mark Goodson. Ryan has also written for **"Password Plus,"** **"Trivia Trap,"** **"Body Language,"** and **"Catch Phrase,"** and created all the rebus puzzles for TV's **"Classic Concentration"** and contributed **"The Price Is Right"** pricing game *Now & Then*. Steve has also created lottery games with million-dollar payoffs for many states and countries around the world.

Ryan is the author of more than twenty popular books, including *Brain Busters, Lunchbox Puzzles, Sit & Solve Pencil Puzzles, Test Your Puzzle IQ, Mystifying Math Puzzles, Great Rebus Puzzles, Classic Concentration* and co-author of *The Encyclopedia of TV Game Shows* and *The Ultimate TV Game Show Book*. His puzzles have also appeared in such magazines as *Games, Nickelodeon* and *World of Puzzles* in the U.S. and *Games & Puzzles* in the United Kingdom. Worldwide, his puzzle books have been translated into Chinese, Dutch, French, Italian, Portuguese, Russian and Spanish and have also surfaced in India, Pakistan and Indonesia with other faraway lands soon to experience Ryan's puzzling world.

Many predicted Ryan's gifts in art, design, and mathematics would lead to a career in architecture. But as usual, Ryan had a surprise twist in store: he built a mental gymnastics empire instead.

Nothing puzzling about that.

For more information visit: www.SteveRyanGames.com.

Puzzle Index

Chapter 1

Chapter 2

Chapter 3

Chapter 4

Page key: **puzzle**, *clue*, solution